F.S.A. Cyril Davenport

English Embroidered Book Bindings

F.S.A. Cyril Davenport

English Embroidered Book Bindings

ISBN/EAN: 9783743481565

Manufactured in Europe, USA, Canada, Australia, Japa

Cover: Foto ©Thomas Meinert / pixelio.de

Manufactured and distributed by brebook publishing software (www.brebook.com)

F.S.A. Cyril Davenport

English Embroidered Book Bindings

EDITED BY
ALFRED POLLARD

ENGLISH EMBROIDERED BOOKBINDINGS

BY CYRIL DAVENPORT, F.S.A.

AUTHOR OF

'THE ENGLISH REGALIA'

ETC.

LONDON
KEGAN PAUL, TRENCH, TRÜBNER
AND COMPANY, LIMITED
1899

The English
Bookman's
Library

CONTENTS AND LIST OF PLATES

GENERAL INTRODUCTION

A NEW series of 'Books about Books,' exclusively English in its aims, may seem to savour of the patriotism which, in matters of art and historical research, is, with reason enough, often scoffed at as a treacherous guide. No doubt in these pleasant studies patriotism acts as a magnifying-glass, making us unduly exaggerate details. On the other hand, it encourages us to try to discover them, and just at present this encouragement seems to be needed. There are so many gaps in our knowledge of the history of books in England that we can hardly claim that our own dwelling is set in order, and yet many of our bookmen appear more inclined to re-decorate their neighbours' houses than to do work that still urgently needs to be done at home. The reasons for this transference of energy are not far to seek. It is quite easy to be struck with the inferiority of English books and their accessories, such as bindings and illustrations, to those produced on the Continent.

b

To compare the books printed by Caxton with the best work of his German or Italian contemporaries, to compare the books bound for Henry, Prince of Wales, with those bound for the Kings of France, to try to find even a dozen English books printed before 1640 with woodcuts (not imported from abroad) of any real artistic merit—if any one is anxious to reinforce his national modesty, here are three very efficacious methods of doing it! On the other hand, English book-collectors have always been cosmopolitan in their tastes, and without leaving England it is possible to study to some effect, in public or private libraries, the finest books of almost any foreign country. It is small wonder, therefore, that our bookmen, when they have been minded to write on their hobbies, have sought beauty and stateliness of work where they could most readily find them, and that the labourers in the book-field of our own country are not numerous. Touchstone's remark, 'a poor thing, but mine own,' might, on the worst view of the case, have suggested greater diligence at home; but on a wider view English book-work is by no means a 'poor thing.' Its excellence at certain periods is as striking as its inferiority at others, and it is a literal fact that there is no art or craft connected with books in which England, at one time or another, has not held the primacy in Europe.

It would certainly be unreasonable to complain that printing with movable types was not invented at a time better suited to our national convenience. Yet the fact that the invention was made just in the middle of the fifteenth century constituted a handicap by which the printing trade in this country was for generations overweighted. At almost any earlier period, more particularly from the beginning of the fourteenth century to the first quarter of the fifteenth, England would have been as well equipped as any foreign country to take its part in the race. From the production of Queen Mary's Psalter at the earlier date to that of the Sherborne Missal at the later, English manuscripts, if we may judge from the scanty specimens which the evil days of Henry VIII. and Edward VI. have left us, may vie in beauty of writing and decoration with the finest examples of Continental art. If John Siferwas, instead of William Caxton, had introduced printing into England, our English incunabula would have taken a far higher place. But the sixty odd years which separate the two men were absolutely disastrous to the English book-trade. After her

exhausting and futile struggle with France, England was torn asunder by the wars of the Roses,
and by the time these were ended the school of
illumination, so full of promise, and seemingly
so firmly established, had absolutely died out.
When printing was introduced England possessed
no trained illuminators or skilful scribes such
as in other countries were forced to make the
best of the new art in order not to lose their
living, nor were there any native wood-engravers
ready to illustrate the new books. I have never
myself seen or heard of a 'Caxton' in which an
illuminator has painted a preliminary border or
initial letters ; even the rubrication, where it exists,
is usually a disfigurement ; while as for pictures,
it has been unkindly said that inquiry whence
they were obtained is superfluous, since any boy
with a knife could have cut them as well.

Making its start under these unfavourable
conditions, the English book-trade was exposed
at once to the full competition of the Continental
presses, Richard III. expressly excluding it from
the protection which was given to other in-
dustries. Practically all learned books of every
sort, the great majority of our service-books,
most grammars for use in English schools, and
even a few popular books of the kind to which

Caxton devoted himself, were produced abroad for the English market and freely imported. Only those who mistake the shadow for the substance will regret this free trade, to which we owe the development of scholarship in England during the sixteenth century. None the less, it was hard on a young industry, and though Pynson, Wynkyn de Worde, the Faques, Berthelet, Wolfe, John Day, and others produced fine books in England during the sixteenth century, the start given to the Continental presses was too great, and before our printers had fully caught up their competitors, they too were seized with the carelessness and almost incredible bad taste which marks the books of the first half of the seventeenth century in every country of Europe.

Towards the close of the eighteenth century, as is well known, the French thought sufficiently well of Baskerville's types to purchase a fount after his death for the printing of an important edition of the works of Voltaire. But the merits of Baskerville as a printer, never very cordially admitted, are now more hotly disputed than ever ; and if I am asked at what period English printing has attained that occasional primacy which I have claimed for our exponents of all the bookish arts,

I would boldly say that it possesses it at the
present day. On the one hand, the Kelmscott
Press books, on their own lines, are the finest
and the most harmonious which have ever been
produced ; on the other, the book-work turned
out in the ordinary way of business by the five
or six leading printers of England and Scotland
seems to me, both in technical qualities and in
excellence of taste, the finest in the world, and
with no rival worth mentioning, except in the
work of one or two of the best firms in the United
States. Moreover, as far as I can learn, it is only
in Great Britain and America that the form of
books is now the subject of the ceaseless experi-
ment and ingenuity which are the signs of a
period of artistic activity.

As regards book-illustration the same claim
may be put forward, though with a little more
hesitation. We have been taught lately, with
insistence, that 'the sixties' marked an epoch
in English art, solely from the black and white
work in illustrated books. At that period our
book-pictures are said to have been the best in
the world ; unfortunately our book-decoration,
whether better or worse than that of other
countries, was almost unmitigatedly bad. In
the last quarter of a century our decorative work

has improved in the most striking manner; our illustrations, if judged merely for their pictorial qualities, have not advanced. In the eyes of artists the sketches for book-work now being produced in other countries are probably as good as our own. But an illustration is not merely a picture, it is a picture to be placed in a certain position in a printed book, and in due relation to the size of the page and the character of the type. English book-illustrators by no means always realise this distinction, yet there is on the whole a greater feeling for these proprieties in English books than in those of other countries, and this is an important point in estimating merits. Another important point is that the rule of the 'tint' or 'half-tone' block, with its inevitable accompaniment of loaded paper, ugly to the eye and heavy in the hand, though it has seriously damaged English illustrated work, has not yet gained the predominance it has in other countries. Our best illustrated books are printed from line-blocks, and there are even signs of a possible revival of artistic wood-engraving.

In endeavouring to make good my assertion of what I have called the occasional primacy of English book-work, I am not unaware of the danger of trying, or seeming to try, to play the

strains of ' Rule Britannia ' on my own poor penny
whistle.   As regards manuscripts, therefore, it
is a pleasure to be able to seek shelter behind
the authority of Sir Edward Maunde Thompson,
whose words in this connection carry all the
more weight, because he has shown himself a
severe critic of the claims which have been put
forward on behalf of several fine manuscripts to
be regarded as English.   In the closing para-
graphs of his monograph on *English Illuminated
Manuscripts* he thus sums up the pretensions of
the English school :—

'The freehand drawing of our artists under the Anglo-Saxon
kings was incomparably superior to the dead copies from Byzan-
tine models which were in favour abroad.   The artistic instinct
was not destroyed, but rather strengthened, by the incoming
of Norman influence ; and of the twelfth and thirteenth centuries
there is abundant material to show that English book-decoration
was then at least equal to that of neighbouring countries.   For
our art of the early fourteenth century we claim a still higher
position, and contend that no other nation could at that time
produce such graceful drawing.   Certainly inferior to this high
standard of drawing was the work of the latter part of that
century ; but still, as we have seen, in the miniatures of this
time we have examples of a rising school of painting which bid
fair to attain to a high standard of excellence, and which only
failed for political causes.'[1]

To this judicial pronouncement on the excel-

[1] *English Illuminated Manuscripts.* By Sir Edward Maunde Thompson,
K.C.B. (Kegan Paul, 1895), pp. 66, 67.

lence of English manuscripts on their decorative
side, we may fairly add the fact that manuscripts
of literary importance begin at an earlier date in
England than in any other country, and that the
Cotton MS. of *Beowulf* and the miscellanies which
go by the names of the *Exeter Book* and the
Vercelli Book have no contemporary parallels in
the rest of Europe.

When we turn from books, printed or in manuscript, to their possessors, it is only just to begin
with a compliment to our neighbours across the
Channel. No English bookman holds the unique
position of Jean Grolier, and 'les femmes biblio-
philes' of England have been few and undistin-
guished compared with those of France. Grolier,
however, and his fair imitators, as a rule, bought
only the books of their own day, giving them
distinction by the handsome liveries which they
made them don. Our English collectors have more
often been of the omnivorous type, and though
Lords Lumley and Arundel in the sixteenth
century cannot, even when their forces are joined,
stand up against De Thou, in Sir Robert Cotton,
Harley, Thomas Rawlinson, Lord Spencer, Heber,
Grenville, and Sir Thomas Phillips (and the list
might be doubled without much relaxation of
the standard), we have a succession of English

collectors to whom it would be difficult to produce
foreign counterparts. Round these *dii majores*
have clustered innumerable demigods of the book-
market, and certainly in no other country has
collecting been as widely diffused, and pursued
with so much zest, as in England during the
present century. It is to be regretted that so
few English collectors have cared to leave their
marks of ownership on the books they have taken
so much pleasure in bringing together. Michael
Wodhull was a model in this respect, for his book-
stamp is one of the most pleasing of English
origin, and his autograph notes recording the
prices he paid for his treasures, and his assiduous
collation of them, make them doubly precious in
the eyes of subsequent owners. Mr. Grenville
also had his book-stamp, though there is little
joy to be won from it, for it is unpleasing in
itself, and is too often found spoiling a fine old
binding. Mr. Cracherode's stamp was as graceful as Wodhull's; but, as a rule, our English
collectors, though, as Mr. Fletcher is discovering,
many more of them than is generally known have
possessed a stamp, have not often troubled to use
it, and their collections have never obtained the
reputation which they deserve, mainly for lack
of marks of ownership to keep them green in

the memory of later possessors. That this should be so in a country where book-plates have been so common may at first seem surprising. But book-plates everywhere have been used rather by the small collectors than the great ones, and the regrettable peculiarity of our English book-men is, not that they despised this rather fugitive sign of possession, but that for the most part they despised book-stamps as well.

Of book-plates themselves I have no claim to speak; but for good taste and grace of design the best English Jacobean and Chippendale specimens seem to me the most pleasing of their kind, and certainly in our own day the work of Mr. Sherborn has no rival, except in that of Mr. French, who, in technique, would, I imagine, not refuse to call himself his disciple.

I have purposely left to the last the subject of Bindings, as this, being more immediately cognate to Mr. Davenport's book, may fairly be treated at rather greater length. If the French dictum ' la reliure est un art tout français ' is not without its historical justification, it is at least possible to show that England has done much admirable work, and that now and again, as in the other bookish arts, she has attained pre-eminence.

The first point which may fairly be made is
that England is the only country besides France
in which the art has been consistently practised.
In Italy, binding, like printing, flourished for a
little over half a century with extraordinary vigour
and grace, and then fell suddenly and completely
from its high estate. From 1465 to the death
of Aldus the books printed in Italy were the
finest in the world; from the beginning of the
work of Aldus to about 1560 Italian bindings
possess a freedom of graceful design which even
the superior technical skill quickly gained by the
French does not altogether outbalance. But just
as after about 1520 a finely printed Italian book
can hardly be met with, so after 1560, save for
a brief period during which certain fan-shaped
designs attained prettiness, there have been no
good Italian bindings. In Germany, when in
the fifteenth century, before the introduction of
gold tooling, there was a thriving school of binders
working in the mediæval manner, the Renaissance
brought with it an absolute decline. Holland,
again, which in the fifteenth century had made
a charming use of large panel stamps, has since
that period had only two binders of any reputation, Magnus and Poncyn, of Amsterdam, who
worked for the Elzéviers and Louis xiv. Of

Spanish bindings few fine specimens have been unearthed, and these are all early. Only England can boast that, like France, she has possessed one school of binders after another, working with varying success from the earliest times down to the present century, in which bookbinding all over Europe has suffered from the servility with which the old designs, now for the first time fully appreciated, have been copied and imitated.

In this length of pedigree it must be noted that England far surpasses even France herself. The magnificent illuminated manuscripts, the finest of their age, which were produced at Winchester during the tenth century, were no doubt bound in the jewelled metal covers of which the rapacity of the sixteenth century has left hardly a single trace in this country. But early in the twelfth century, if not before, the Winchester bookmen turned their attention also to leather binding, and the school of design which they started, spreading to Durham, London, and Oxford, did not die out in England until it was ousted by the large panel stamps introduced from France at the end of the fifteenth. The predominant feature of these Winchester bindings (of which a fine example from the library of William Morris recently sold for £180), and of

their successors, is the employment of small
stamps, from half an inch to an inch in size,
sometimes circular, more often square or pear-
shaped, and containing figures, grotesques, or
purely conventional designs. A circle, or two
half-circles, formed by the repetition of one stamp,
within one or more rectangles formed by others,
is perhaps the commonest scheme of decoration,
but it is the characteristic of these bindings, as of
the finest in gold tooling, that by the repetition
of a few small patterns an endless variety of
designs could be built up. The British Museum
possesses a few good examples of this stamp-
work, but the finest collections of them are in
the Cathedral libraries at Durham and Hereford.
Any one, however, who is interested in this work
can easily acquaint himself with it by consulting
the unique collection of rubbings carefully taken
by Mr. Weale and deposited in the National Art
Library at the South Kensington Museum. In
these rubbings, as in no other way, the history of
English binding can be studied from the earliest
Winchester books to the charming Oxford bindings executed by Thomas Hunt, the English
partner of the Cologne printer, Rood, about 1481.

During the first half of this period the English
leather binders were the finest in Europe ; during

the second, the Germans pressed them hard, and when the large panel stamps, three or four inches square and more, were introduced in Holland and France, the English adaptations of them were distinctly inferior to the originals. The earliest English bindings with gold tooling were, of course, also imitative. The use of gold reached this country but slowly, as the first known English binding, in which it occurs, is on a book printed in 1541, by which time the art had been common in Italy for a generation. The English bindings found on books bound for Henry VIII., Edward VI., and Mary I., all of which are roughly assigned to Berthelet as the Royal binder, resemble the current Italian designs of the day, with sufficient differences to make it probable that they were produced by Englishmen. We know, however, that until the close of the century there were occasional complaints of the presence of foreign binders in London, and it is probable that the Grolieresque bindings executed for Wotton were foreign rather than English. Where, however, we find work on English books distinctly unlike anything in France or Italy, it is reasonable to assign it to a native school, and such a school seems to have grown up about 1570, in the workshop of John Day, the helper of

Archbishop Parker in so many of his literary
undertakings. These bindings attributed to Day,
especially those in which he worked with white
leather on brown, although they have none of the
French delicacy of tooling, perhaps for this reason
attack the problem of decoration with a greater
sense of the difference between the styles suitable
for a large book and a small than is always found
in France, where the greatest binders, such as
Nicholas Eve and Le Gascon, often covered large
folios with endless repetitions of minute tools
whose full beauty can only be appreciated on
duodecimos or octavos. The English designs
with a large centre ornament and corner-pieces are
rich and impressive, and we may fairly give Day
and his fellows the palm for originality and effectiveness among Elizabethan binders. In the
next reign the French use of the semé or powder,
a single small stamp, of a fleur-de-lys, a thistle, a
crown, or the like, impressed in rows all over the
cover, was increasingly imitated in England, very
unsuccessfully, and, save for a few traces of the
style of Day, the leather bindings of the first third
of the century deserve the worst epithets which
can be given them.

Until, however, French fashions came into
vogue after the Restoration, English binders had

never been content to regard leather as the sole
material in which they could work. Embroidered
bindings had come early into use in England, and
a Psalter embroidered by Anne Felbrigge towards
the close of the fourteenth century is preserved
at the British Museum, and shown in one of Mr.
Davenport's illustrations. In the sixteenth century
embroidered work was very popular with the
Tudor princesses, gold and silver thread and
pearls being largely used, often with very decorative effect. The simplest of these covers are also
the best—but great elaboration was often employed, and on a presentation copy of Archbishop
Parker's *De Antiquitate Ecclesiæ Britannicæ*
we find a clever but rather grotesque representation of a deer-paddock. Under the Stuarts the
lighter feather-stitch was preferred, and there
seems to have been a regular trade in embroidered
Bibles and Prayer-books of small size, sometimes
with floral patterns, sometimes with portraits of
the King, or Scriptural scenes. A dealer's freak
which compelled the British Museum to buy a
pair of elaborate gloves of the period rather than
lose a finely embroidered Psalter, with which they
went, was certainly a fortunate one, enabling us
to realise that in hands thus gloved these little
bindings, always pretty, often really artistic, must

d

have looked exactly right, while their vivid colours must have been admirably in harmony with the gay Cavalier dresses.

Besides furnishing a ground for embroidery, velvet bindings were often decorated, in England, with goldsmith work. One of the most beautiful little bookcovers in existence is on a book of prayers, bound for Queen Elizabeth in red velvet, with a centre and corner pieces delicately enamelled on gold. Under the Stuarts, again, we frequently find similar ornaments in engraved silver, and their charm is incontestable.

Thus while for English bindings of this period in gilt leather we can only claim that Berthelet's show some freedom in their adaptation of Italian models, and Day's a more decided originality, we are entitled to set side by side with this scanty record a host of charming bindings in more feminine materials, which have no parallel in France, and certainly deserve some recognition. After the Restoration, however, leather quickly ousted its competitors, and a school of designers and gilders arose in England, which, while taking its first inspiration from Le Gascon, soon developed an individual style. In effectiveness, though not in minute accuracy of execution, this may rank with the best in Europe. We can trace the beginnings of this lighter and most graceful work as early as the thirties, and it might be contended with a certain plausibility that it began at the Universities. Certainly the two earliest examples known to me—the copy of her *Statutes* presented to Charles I. by Oxford in 1634, and the Little Gidding *Harmony* of 1635, the tools employed in which have been shown by Mr. Davenport to have been used also by Buck, of Cambridge—are two of the finest English bindings in existence, and in both cases, despite the multiplicity of the tiny tools employed, there is a unity and largeness of design which, as I have ventured to hint, is not always found even in the best French work. The chief English bindings after the Restoration, those associated with the name of Samuel Mearne, the King's Binder, preserve this character, though the attempt to break the formality of the rectangle by the bulges at the side and the little penthouses at foot and head (whence its name, the 'cottage' style) was not wholly successful. The use of the labour-saving device of the 'roll,' in preference to impressing each section of the pattern by hand, is another blot. Nevertheless, it is almost impossible to find an English or Scotch binding of this period which is less than charming, and the best of them are admirable. At the beginning of

the eighteenth century a new grace was added
by the inlaying of a leather of a second colour.
These inlaid English bindings are few in number
(the British Museum has not a single fine example),
but those who know the specimens exhibited at
the Burlington Fine Arts Club, two of which are
figured in its Catalogue, will readily allow that
their grace has never been surpassed. The fine
Harleian bindings let us down gently from this
eminence, and then, after a period of mere dul-
ness, with the rise of Roger Payne we have again
an English school (for Payne's traditions were
worthily followed by Charles Lewis) which, by
common consent, was the finest of its time.
Payne's originality is, perhaps, not quite so absolute as has been maintained, for some of his
tools were cut in the pattern of Mearne's, and it
would be possible to find suggestions for some of
his schemes of arrangement in earlier English
work. If he borrowed, however, he borrowed
from his English predecessors, and he brought
to his task an individuality and an artistic instinct which cannot be denied.

  After Payne and Lewis, English binding, like
French, became purely imitative in its designs;
but while in our own decade the French artists
have endeavoured to shake themselves free from

old traditions by mere eccentricity, in England we have several living binders, such as Mr. Cobden Sanderson and Mr. Douglas Cockerell, who work with notable originality and yet with the strictest observance of the canons of their art.

Moreover in the application of decorative designs to cloth cases England has invented, and England and America have brought to perfection, an inexpensive and very pleasing form of book-cover, which gives the bookman ample time to consider whether his purchase is worth the more permanent honours of gilded leather, and also, by the facts that it is avowedly temporary, and that its decoration is cheaply and easily effected by large stamps, renders forgivable vagaries of de-sign, which when translated, as they have been of late years in France, into the time-honoured and solemn leather, seem merely incongruous and irreverent.

In binding, then, as in the other bookish arts, the part which English workers have played has been no insignificant or unworthy one, and the development of this art, as of the others, in our own country is worthy of study. In this case much has already been done, for the illustrations of *English Bookbindings at the British Museum*, edited, with introduction and descriptions by Mr.

W. Y. Fletcher, present the student with the best possible survey of the whole subject, while the excellent treatises of Miss Prideaux and Mr. Horne bring English bookbinding into relation with that of other countries. Here, then, there is no need of a new general history, but rather of special monographs, treating more in detail of the periods at which our English binders have done the best work. The old stamped bindings of the days of manuscript, the embroidered bindings of the sixteenth and seventeenth centuries, the leather bindings of Mearne and his fellows under the later Stuarts, and the work of Roger Payne— all these seem to offer excellent subjects for unpretentious monographs, and it is hoped that others of them besides the *English Embroidered Bindings*, with which Mr. Davenport has made a beginning, may be treated in this series.

In other subjects the ground has not yet been cleared to the same extent, and for the history of English Book-Collectors and English Printing, not special monographs, but good general surveys are the first need. To say much on this subject might bring me perilously near to re-writing the prospectus of this series. It is enough to have pointed out that the bookish arts in England are well worth more study than they have yet been

CHAPTER I

THE application of needlework to the embellishment of the bindings of books has hitherto almost escaped special notice. In most of the works on the subject of English Bookbinding, considered from the decorative point of view in distinction from the technical, a few examples of embroidered covers have indeed received some share of attention. Thus in both Mr. H. B. Wheatley's and Mr. W. Y. Fletcher's works on the bindings in the British Museum, in Mr. Salt Brassington's *Historic Bindings in the Bodleian Library* and *History of the Art of Bookbinding*, and in my own *Portfolio* monograph on 'Royal English Bookbindings,' some of the finer specimens of embroidered books still existing are illustrated and described. But up to the present no attempt has been made to deal with them as a separate subject. In the course, however, of the many lectures on Decorative Bookbinding which it has been my pleasure and honour to deliver during

A

the past few years, I have invariably noticed that
the pictures and descriptions of embroidered
specimens have been the most keenly appreciated,
and this favourable sign has led me to examine
and consider such examples as have come in my
way more carefully than I might otherwise have
done. Very little study sufficed to show that in
England alone there was for a considerable
period a regular and large production of embroidered books, and further, that the different
styles of these embroideries are clearly defined,
equally from the chronological and artistic points
of view. A peculiarly English art which thus
lends itself to orderly treatment may fairly be
made the subject of a brief monograph.

With the exception of point-lace, which is sometimes made in small pieces for such purposes as
ladies' cuffs or collars, decorative work produced
by the aid of the needle is generally large. Certainly this is so in its finest forms, which are
probably to be found in the ecclesiastical vest-
ments and in the altar frontals of the Renaissance
period, or even earlier. On the other hand, such
work as exists on books is always of small size,
and, unlike the point-lace, it almost invariably has
more than one kind of ' stitchery ' upon it—chain,
split, tapestry, satin, or what not.

Thus it can be claimed as a distinction for
embroidered book-covers that as a class they
are the smallest complete embroideries existing,

ranging upwards from about 6 inches by 3½ inches—the size of the smallest specimen known to me, when opened out to its fullest extent, sides and back in one. This covers a copy of the Psalms, printed in London in 1635, and is of white satin, with a small tulip worked in coloured silk on each side.

An 'Embroidered Book,' it should be said, means for my purpose a book which is covered, sides and back, by a piece of material ornamented with needlework, following a design made for the purpose of adorning that particular book. A cover consisting of merely a piece of woven stuff, or even a piece of true embroidery cut from a larger piece, is not, from my point of view, properly to be considered an 'embroidered book,' it being essential that the design as well as the workmanship should have been specially made for the book on which they are found ; and this, in the large majority of instances, is certainly the case.

With regard to the transference of bindings to books other than those for which they were originally made, such a transference has often taken place in the case of mediæval books bound in ornamental metal, but even in these instances it must be recognised that such a change can seldom be made without serious detriment. It is chiefly indeed from some incongruity of style or technical mistake in the re-putting together that we are led to guess that the covers have been thus tampered with. Now and then such a transference occurs in the case of leather-bound books, and in such instances is usually easy for a trained binder to detect. Embroidered covers, on the other hand, have rarely been changed, the motive for such a proceeding never having been strong, and the risk attending it being obvious enough. We may, in fact, feel tolerably sure that the large majority of embroidered covers still remain on the boards of the books they were originally made for.

All the embroidered books now extant dating from before the reign of Queen Elizabeth have gone through the very unfortunate operation of ' re-backing,' in the course of which the old embroidered work is replaced by new leather. The old head and tail bands, technically very interesting, have been replaced by modern imitations, and considerable damage has been done in distorting the work left on the sides of the book. It would seem obvious that a canvas, velvet, or satin embroidered binding, if it really must be re-backed or repaired at all, should be mended with a material as nearly as possible of the same make and colour as that of the original covering; but this has rarely been done, the large majority of such repairs being executed in leather. But in the case of such old bindings we must be grateful for small mercies, and feel thankful that even the sides are left in so many cases. It is indeed surprising that we still possess as much as we do. If all our great collectors had been of the same mind as Henry Prince of Wales, the Right Hon. Thomas Grenville, or even King George III., we should have been far worse off, as although several fine old bindings exist in their libraries, many which would now be priceless have been destroyed, only to be replaced by comparatively modern bindings, sometimes the best of their kind, but often in bad taste.

Division of Embroidered Books according to the designs upon them.

The designs on embroidered books may be roughly divided into four classes — Heraldic, Figure, Floral, and Arabesque.

The Heraldic designs always denote ownership, and are most frequently found on Royal books bound in velvet, rarely occurring on silk or satin, and never, as far as I have been able to ascertain, on canvas. The Figure designs may be subdivided into three smaller classes, viz.:—

    I. Scriptural, *e.g.* representations of Solomon and the Queen of Sheba, Jacob wrestling with the Angel, David, etc.

    II. Symbolical, *e.g.* figures of Faith, Hope, Peace, Plenty, etc.

    III. Portraits, *e.g.* of Charles I., Queen Henrietta Maria, Duke of Buckingham, etc.

The Scriptural designs are most generally found on canvas-bound books; the Symbolical figures, and Portraits, on satin, rarely on velvet. The Floral and Arabesque designs are most common on small and unimportant works bound in satin, but they occur now and then on both canvas and velvet books. The true arabesques have no animal or insect forms among them, the prophet Mohammed having forbidden his followers to imitate any living thing.

It may further be noted that heraldic designs on embroidered books are early, having been made chiefly during the sixteenth century, and that the figure, floral, and arabesque designs most usually belong to the seventeenth century. There are, of course, exceptions to these divisions, notably in the case of the earliest existing embroidered book, which has figure designs on both sides, but also maintains its heraldic position, inasmuch as its edges are decorated with coats-of-arms.

Naturally, again, it may be sometimes difficult to decide whether a design should be classed as heraldic or floral. Such a difficulty occurs as to the large Bible at Oxford bound in red velvet for Queen Elizabeth, and bearing a design of Tudor and York roses. I consider it heraldic, but it might, with no less appropriateness, be called floral. If it had belonged to any one not a member of the Royal family it would undoubtedly be properly counted as a floral specimen. Again,

in many of the portrait bindings flowers and
arabesques are introduced, but they are clearly
subordinate, and the chief decorative motive of
such designs must be looked for, and the work
classed accordingly. Thus it is evident that the
arrangement of the embroidered books by their
designs cannot be too rigidly applied, although it
should not be lost sight of altogether.

*Division of Embroidered Books according to the
material on which they are worked.*

A more useful and accurate classification may
however be found by help of the material on
which the embroidered work is done, and this
division is obvious and easy. With very few
exceptions all embroidered books, ancient and
modern, are worked on *canvas, velvet,* or *satin,*
and while canvas was used continuously from
the fourteenth century until the middle of the
seventeenth century, velvet was most largely used
during the Tudor period, and satin during that
of the early Stuarts.

Broadly speaking, the essential differences in
the kind of work found upon these three materials
follow the peculiarities of the materials themselves. Canvas, in itself of no decorative value,
is always completely covered with needlework.
Velvet, beautiful even when alone, but difficult
to work upon, usually has a large proportion of

appliqué, laid, or couched work, in coloured silk
or satin, upon it, showing always large spaces
unworked upon, and such actual work as occurs
directly on the velvet is always in thick guimp
or gold cord.　Satin, equally beautiful in its way,
is also freely left unornamented in places; the
needlework directly upon it is often very fine and
delicate in coloured floss silks, generally closely
protected by thick raised frames or edges of
metallic threads or fine gold or silver cords.

FIG. 1.
Silken thread closely
wound round with
strip of flat metal.

FIG. 2.
Silken thread loosely
wound round with
strip of flat metal.

FIG. 3.
Strips of flat metal cut into
shapes and kept down by
small stitches at regular intervals.　Called ' Lizzarding.'

By 'metallic' threads, when they are not
simply fine wires, I mean strands of silk
closely (Fig. 1) or loosely (Fig. 2) wound round
with narrow coils of thin metal, mostly silver or
silver gilt.　The use of such threads, alone, or
twisted into cords, is common on all styles of embroidered books, and it is largely due to their use
that pieces of work apparently of the greatest
delicacy are really extremely durable—far more

so than is generally supposed. Certainly if it had not been for the efficient protection of these little metal walls we should not possess, as we actually do, delicate-looking embroidered books, hundreds of years old, in almost as good condition, except in the matter of colour, as when they were originally made.

Thin pieces of metal are sometimes used alone, caught down at regular intervals by small cross stitches; this is, I believe, called 'Lizzarding' (Fig. 3). Metal is also found in the form of 'guimp,' in flattened spirals (Fig. 4), and also in the 'Purl,' or copper wire covered with silk (Fig. 5), so common on the later satin books (compare p. 46).

FIG. 4.
Edging made with a piece of spiral wire hammered flat, appearing like a series of small rings.

FIG. 5.
Loop made of a short length of Purl threaded, the ends drawn together.

Spangles appear to have been introduced during the reign of Elizabeth, but they were never freely used on velvet, finding their proper place ultimately on the satin books of a later time. The spangles are generally kept in position either by a small section of purl (Fig. 6) or a seed pearl (Fig. 7), in both cases very efficaciously, so that the use of guimp or pearl was not only ornamental but served the same protective purpose as the bosses on a shield, or those so commonly

B

found upon the sides of the stamped leather bindings of mediæval books.

FIG. 6.	FIG. 7.	FIG. 8.
Spangle kept in place by a stitch through a short piece of Purl.	Spangle kept in place by a stitch through a seed pearl.	Binder's stamp for gold tooling, cut in imitation of a spangle.

It may be mentioned that the seventeenth-
century Dutch binders, Magnus and Poncyn,
both of Amsterdam, invented a new tool for
gilding on leather bindings, used, of course, in
combination with others. This was cut to imitate
the small circular spangles of the embroidered
books (Fig. 8), and the English and French finishers
of a later period used the same device with excellent effect for filling up obtrusive spaces on the
sides and backs of their decorative bindings.
Thus it may be taken as an axiom that, for the
proper working of an embroidered book, except it
be tapestry-stitch or tent-stitch, on canvas, which
is flat and strong of itself, there should invariably
be a liberal use of metal threads, these being not
only very decorative in themselves, but also pro-
viding a valuable protection to the more delicate
needlework at a lower level, and to the material
of the ground itself.

The earliest examples of embroidered bindings
still existing are not by any means such as would
lead to the inference that they were exceptional
productions—made when the idea of the applica-

tion of needlework to the decoration of books was
in its infancy. On the contrary, they are instances
of very skilled workmanship, so that it is probable
that the art was practised at an earlier date
than we now have recorded. There are, indeed,
frequent notes in 'Wardrobe Accounts' and else-
where of books bound in velvet and satin at a
date anterior to any now existing, but there is no
mention of embroidered work upon them.

The Forwarding of Embroidered Books.

The processes used in the binding of embroidered books are the same as in the case of
leather-bound books; but there is one invariable
peculiarity—the bands upon which the different
sections of the paper are sewn are never in relief,
so that it was always possible to paste down a
piece of material easily along the back without
having to allow for the projecting bands so
familiar on leather bindings (Fig. 9). The backs,
moreover, are only rounded very slightly, if at all.

This flatness has been attained on the earlier
books either by sewing on flat bands, thin strips
of leather or vellum (Fig. 10), or by flattening
the usual hempen bands as much as they will
bear by the hammer, and afterwards filling up
the intermediate spaces with padding of some
suitable material, linen or thin leather.

In several instances the difficulty of flattening the bands has been solved, in sixteenth- and

seventeenth-century embroidered books, in a way which cannot be too strongly condemned from a constructive point of view, although it has served its immediate purpose admirably.

A small trench has been cut with a sharp knife for each band, deep enough to sink it to the general level of the inner edges of the sections (Fig. 11).

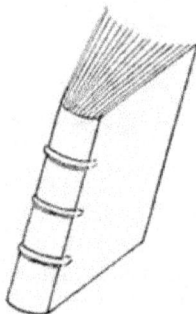

FIG. 9.
Back of book sewn on raised bands.

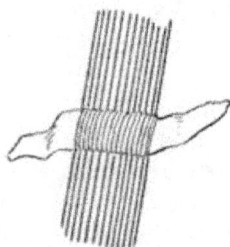

FIG. 10.
Band of flat vellum sometimes found on old books with flat backs.

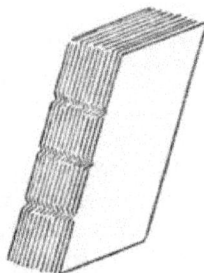

FIG. 11.
Typical appearance of a book, before it is sewn, with small trenches cut in the back in which the bands are to be laid; a bad method, but often used to produce a flat back.

This cutting of the back to make room for the bands was afterwards more easily effected by means of a saw—as it is done now—and in the eighteenth century was especially used by the French binder Derome le Jeune, who is usually made responsible for its invention.

The existence of the sunken bands on early embroidered books probably marks the beginning

of this vicious system, but here there is some
excuse for it, whereas in the case of ordinary
leather-bound books there is none, except from
the commercial standpoint.

In the case of vellum books there may be
some reason for using the 'sawn in' bands, as it
is certainly difficult to get vellum to fit comfort-
ably over raised bands, although numerous early
instances exist in which it has been successfully
done.   Again in the case of 'hollow backs,' the
bands are kept flat with some reason.   But for
all valuable or finely bound books the system of
'sawing in' cannot be too strongly condemned.

'Sawing in' can be detected by looking at the
threads in the centre of any section of a bound
book from the inside.   It will show as a small hole
with a piece of hemp or leather lying transversely
across it, under which the thread passes (Fig. 12).

FIG. 12.

Typical appearance of the sewing of a book with 'sawn in' bands, as
seen from the inside of each section.   The bands just visible.

In the case of a properly sewn book, the bands themselves cannot be seen at all from the inside of the sections, unless, indeed, the book is damaged (Fig. 13). If the covering of the back

FIG. 13.

Typical appearance of the sewing of a book on raised bands, as seen from the inside of each section. The bands invisible. Known as 'flexible.'

is off, or even loose, the method of sewing that has been used can very easily be seen; and if it appears that the bands are sunk in a small trench, that is the form of sewing that is called 'sawn in,' or analogous to it.

Although in the embroidered books the bands of the backs do not show on the surface, it is common enough to find the lines they probably follow indicated in the work on the back, which is divided into panels by as many transverse lines, braid or cord, as there are bands underneath them. But in some cases the designer has used the back as one long panel, and decorated

it accordingly as one space. The headbands in
some of the earlier books were sewn at the same
time as the other bands on the sewing-press and
drawn in to the boards, but in most early bindings the ravaging repairer has been at work and
made it impossible to know for certain what
was the state of the headbands before the book
came into his hands. Most of the existing head-
bands are made by hand in the usual way, with
the ends simply cut off, not indeed a very satisfactory finish. It would be better if these ends
were somehow drawn in to the leather of the
back, as for instance they still often are on thin
vellum books.

The great majority of embroidered books, both
large and small, have had ties of silk on their
front edges—generally two, but sometimes only
one, which wraps round. These ties have generally worn away from the outer side of the boards,
but their ends can usually be traced (if the book
has not been repaired) in the inner side, covered
only by a thin piece of paper; and if this paper
is loose, as often happens, and the ends show
well, it may often be advisable not to paste it
down again at that particular place.

The backs of old embroidered books are by
far the weakest parts about them. If they exist
at all in their old forms they are always much
worn, and the work upon them so much damaged
that it is often difficult to make out even the

general character of the design, to say nothing of the details of the workmanship.

The edges of the leaves of books bound in England in embroidered bindings are always ornamentally treated, sometimes simply gilded, often further adorned with 'gauffred' work, that is to say, small patterns impressed on the gold, and sometimes beautifully decorated with elaborate designs having colour in parts as well. The earliest English ornamentation of this kind in colour is found on the Felbrigge Psalter and on some of the books embroidered for Henry VIII., one of which is richly painted on the fore edges with heraldic designs, and another with a motto written in gold on a delicately coloured ground.

Cases for Embroidered Books.

Common though the small satin embroidered books must have been in England during the earlier part of the seventeenth century, it is still certain that the finer specimens were highly prized, and beautifully worked bags were often made for their protection. These bags are always of canvas, and most of them are decorated in the same way, the backgrounds of silver thread with a design in tapestry- or tent-stitch, and having ornamental strings and tassels. To describe one of these is almost to describe all. The best preserved specimen I know belongs to a little satin embroidered

1 Embroidered Bag for Psalms. London, 1633.

copy of the Psalms, printed in London in 1633, and measures 5 inches long by 4 inches in depth.

The same design is repeated on each side. A parrot on a small grass-plot is in the middle of the lower edge. Behind the bird grow two curving stems of thick gold braid, each curve containing a beautifully-worked flower or fruit. In the centre is a carnation, and round it are arranged consecutively a bunch of grapes, a pansy, a honeysuckle, and a double rose, green leaves occurring at intervals. From the lower edge depend three ornamental tassels of silver loops, with small acorns in silver and coloured silks, one from the centre and one from each corner.

The top edge has two draw-strings of gold and red braid, each ending in an ornamental oval acorn of silver thread and coloured silks, probably worked on canvas over a wooden core, ending in a tassel similar to those on the lower edge.

A long loop of gold and silver braid serves as a handle, or means of attachment to a belt, and is fixed at each side near a strong double loop of silver thread, used when pulling the bag open. The lining is of pink silk. This particular bag is perfect in colour as well as condition, but usually the silver has turned black, or nearly so. Besides these very ornamental bags, others of quite simple workmanship are occasionally found, worked in outline with coloured silks. As well as the embroidered bags, certain rectangular cloths

c

variously ornamented, some richly, some plainly, were made and used for the protection of embroidered books, when being read. These, like the bags, only seem to have been used during the seventeenth century. A particularly fine example belongs to a New Testament bound in embroidered satin in 1640. It is of fine linen, measuring 16½ by 9¼ inches, and is beautifully embroidered in a floral design, with thick stalks of gold braid arranged in curves and bearing conventional flowers and leaves, all worked in needle-point lace with coloured silks in a wonderfully skilful manner.

In the centre is a double red rose with separate petals, and among the other flowers are cornflowers, honeysuckles, carnations, strawberries, and several leaves, all worked in the same way, and appliqués at their edges. Some, however, of the larger leaves and petals are ornamentally fastened down to the linen by small coloured stitches arranged in lines or patterns over their surfaces, as well as by the edge stitches. There are several spangles scattered about in the spaces on the linen, and the edge is bound with green silk and gold. On the book itself to which this cover belongs there is a good deal of the same needle-point work, probably executed by the same hand; but the cover is a finer piece altogether than the book,—in fact it is the finest example of such work I have ever seen.

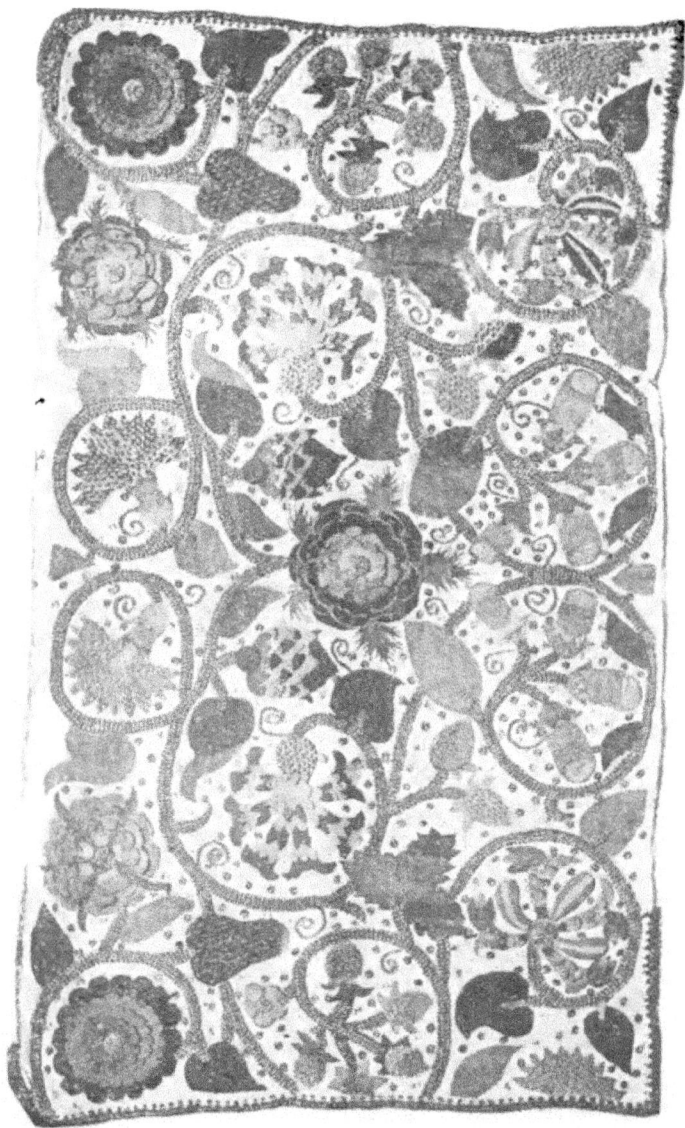

2—Embroidered Cover for New Testament.   London, 1640.

Abroad there have been made at various times embroidered bindings for books, but in no country except England has there been any regular production of them. I have come across a few cases in England of foreign work, the most important of which I will shortly describe. In the British Museum is an interesting specimen bound in red satin, and embroidered with the arms of Felice Peretti, Cardinal de Montalt, who was afterwards Pope Sixtus v.; the coat-of-arms has a little coloured silk upon it, but the border and the cardinal's hat with tassels are all outlined in gold cord. The work is of an elementary character. The book itself is a beautiful illuminated vellum copy of Fichet's *Rhetoric*, printed in Paris in 1471, and presented to the then Pope, Sixtus IV. In the same collection are a few more instances of Italian embroidered bindings, always heraldic in their main designs, the workmanship not being of any particular excellence or character. Perhaps altogether the most interesting Italian work of this kind was done on books bound for Cardinal York, several of which still remain, embroidered with his coat-of-arms, one of them being now in the Royal Library at Windsor. Although the actual workmanship on these books is foreign, we may perhaps claim them as having been suggested or made by the order of the English Prince himself, inheriting the liking for embroidered books from his Stuart ancestors.

French embroidered books are very rare, and I do not know of any examples in England. Two interesting specimens, at least, are in the Bibliothèque Nationale, and are described and figured in Bouchot's work on the artistic bindings in that library. The earlier is on a book of prayers of the fifteenth century, bound in canvas, and worked with 'tapisserie de soie au petit point,' or as I should call it, tent-, or tapestry-, stitch. It represents the Crucifixion and a saint, but M. Bouchot remarks of it, 'La composition est grossière et les figures des plus rudimentaires.'

The other instance occurs on a sixteenth-century manuscript, 'Les Gestes de Blanche de Castille.' It is bound in black velvet, much worn, and ornamented with appliqué embroideries in coloured silks, in shading stitch, probably done on fine linen. The design on the upper cover shows the author of the book, Etienne le Blanc, in the left-hand corner, kneeling at the feet of Louise de Savoie, Regent of France, to whom the book is dedicated. Near her is a fountain into which an antlered stag is jumping, pursued by three hounds.

The Dutch, in the numerous excellent styles of bindings they have so freely imitated from other nations, have not failed to include the English embroidered books. In the South Kensington Museum is a charming specimen of their work on satin, finely worked in coloured silks with small masses of pearls in a rather too elaborate design of flowers and animals. In the British Museum, besides other instances of Dutch needlework, there is a very handsome volume of the *Acta Synodalis Nationalis Dordrechti habitæ*, printed at Leyden in 1620, and bound in crimson velvet. It has the royal coat-of-arms of England within the Garter, with crest, supporters, and motto, all worked in various kinds of gold thread ; in the corners are sprays of roses and thistles alternately, and above and below the coat are the crowned initials J. R., all worked in gold thread.

Hints for Modern Broiderers.

Many book-covers have been embroidered during the last few years in England by ladies working on their own account, or by some of the students at one or other of the many excellent centres now existing for the study and practice of the fascinating art of bookbinding.

Although a large proportion of modern work of this kind has been only copied from older work, I see no reason why original designs should not be freely and successfully invented. But I think that the ancient work may be advantageously studied and carefully copied as far as choice of threads and manner of working them goes. The workers of our old embroidered books were people of great skill and large experience, and from a long and careful examination of much of their work, I am impressed with the conviction that they worked on definite principles. If I allude briefly to some of these I may perhaps give intending workwomen a hint or two as to some minor points which may assist their work to show to the best advantage when *in situ*, and also insure, as far as possible, that it will not be unduly damaged during the operation of fixing to the back and boards of the book for which it is intended.

(1) Before the operation of fixing on the book is begun, it will always be found best to mount the embroidered work on a backing of strong fine linen. The stage at which it is best to add the linen will vary according to the kind of work it is to strengthen. In the case of canvas it will only be necessary to tack it on quite at the last; with velvet a backing from the first may be used with advantage, all the stitches being taken through both materials. As to satin, it will be best to do all the very fine work, if any, in coloured silks first, and when the stronger work in cord or braid comes on, the linen may be then added. The value of the linen is twofold: it strengthens the entire work and protects the finer material from the paste with which it is ultimately fastened on to the book.

(2) A book must be sewn, the edges cut, and

the boards fixed, before the sizes of the sides and back can be accurately measured. These sizes must be given to the designer most carefully, as a very small difference between the real size and the embroidered size will entirely spoil the finished effect, however fine the details of the workmanship may be. When the exact size is known the designer will fill the spaces at his disposal according to his taste and skill, making his sketches on paper, and, when these are complete, transferring the outlines to the material on which the work is to be done. If the designer is also to be the worker it is artistically right, and he, or she, will put in the proper stitches as the work progresses ; but if another person is to execute the needlework it will be best that very detailed description of all the threads and stitches that are to be used should be given, as every designer of an embroidery design intends it to be carried out in a particular way, and unless this way is followed, the design does not have full justice done to it.

(3) In the working itself the greatest care must be taken, especially as to two points : the first and perhaps the more important, because the more difficult to remedy, is that the needlework on the *under* side of the material must be as small and flat as possible, and all knots, lumps, or irregularities here, if they cannot be avoided or safely cut off, had best be brought to the upper side and

worked over. With satin, especially, attention to this point is most necessary, as unless the plain spaces lie quite flat, which they are very apt not to do, the proper appearance of the finished work is spoiled, and however good it may be in all other points, can never be considered first-rate.

The second pitfall to avoid is any pulling or straining of the material during the operation of embroidering it. Success in avoiding this depends primarily upon the various threads being drawn at each stitch to the proper tension, so that it may just have the proper pull to keep it in its place and no more—and although a stitch too loose is bad enough, one too tight is infinitely worse.

(4) The preponderance of appliqué work, and raised work in metal guimps on embroidered books, especially on velvet, is easily accounted for when the principles they illustrate are understood, the truth being that in both these operations the maximum of surface effect is produced with the minimum of under work.

If the piece appliqué is not very large, a series of small stitches along all the edges is generally enough to keep it firm; such edge stitches are in most cases afterwards masked by a gold cord laid over them. If, however, the appliqué piece is large it will be necessary to fix it as well with some supplementary stitches through the central portions. These stitches will generally be so managed that they fit in with, or under, some of the ornamental work; at the same time, if necessary, they may be symmetrically arranged so as to become themselves of a decorative character.

The Embroidered Books here illustrated.

For the purposes of illustration I have chosen the most typical specimens possible from such collections as I have had access to. The chief collections in England are, undoubtedly, those at the British Museum and at the Bodleian Library at Oxford. The collection at the British Museum is especially rich, the earlier and finer specimens almost invariably having formed part of the old Royal Library of England given by George II. to the Museum in 1757.

The more recent specimens have been acquired either by purchase or donation, but as there has been no special intention at any time to collect these bindings, it is remarkable that such a number of them exist in our National Library. The Bodleian is rich in a few fine specimens only, and most of these are exhibited. My illustrations are made from photographs from the books themselves in all instances; to show them properly, however, all should be in colour, and it should not be forgotten that an embroidered book represented only by a half-tint print, however good, inevitably loses its

D

greatest charm. However, if the half-tint is unworthy, the colour prints are distinctly flattering.
I think that almost any old book well reproduced
in colour gains in appearance, and in two of my
colour plates I have actually restored some parts.
In the beautiful fourteenth century psalter, supposed to have been worked by Anne de Felbrigge,
I have made the colours purposely much clearer
than they are at present. If it were possible to
clean this volume, the colours would show very
nearly as they do on my plate; but, actually, they
are all much darker and more indistinct, being in
fact overlaid with the accumulated dirt of centuries.
The other instance where I have added more than
at present exists on the original is the green velvet
book which belonged to Queen Elizabeth, and
forms my frontispiece. Here I have put in the
missing pearls, each of which has left its little
impression on the velvet, so nothing is added for
which there is not the fullest authority. Moreover, some of the gold cord is gone on each of the
three volumes of this work, but I have put it in
its proper place for the purpose of illustration.
The other plates are not in any way materially
altered, but it may be allowed that the colour
plates show their originals at their best.

The books illustrated are selected out of a
large number, and I think it may fairly be considered that the most favourable typical specimens
now left in England are shown. It may well be

that a few finer instances than I have been able
to find may still be discovered hidden away in
private collections, but it is now so rarely that a
really fine ancient embroidered book comes into
the sale-room, that we may safely conclude the
best of them are already safely housed in one or
other of our great national collections.   Where
not otherwise stated, the specimens described are
in the British Museum.

In the following detailed descriptions I have
used the words 'sides' and 'boards' to mean the
same thing, and the measurements refer to the
size of the boards themselves, not including the
back.   These measurements must be taken as ap-
proximate only, as from wear and other causes
the actual sizes would only be truly given by the
use of small fractions of inches.

CHAPTER II

BOOKS BOUND IN CANVAS

ENGLISH books bound in embroidered canvas range over a period of about two hundred and fifty years, the earliest known specimen dating from the fourteenth century, and instances of the work occurring with some frequency from this time until the middle of the seventeenth century. The majority of these bindings are worked in tapestry-stitch, or tent-stitch, in designs illustrating Scriptural subjects in differently coloured threads.

Very often the outlines of these designs are marked by gold threads and cords, of various kinds, and parts of the work are also frequently enriched with further work upon them in metal threads. Spangles are very rarely found on canvas-bound books. The backgrounds of several of the later specimens are worked in silver threads, sometimes in chain-stitch and sometimes in tapestry-stitch ; others again have the ground-

3—The Felbrigge Psalter. 13th-century MS.

work of silver threads laid along the surface of the canvas and caught down at regular intervals by small stitches—this kind of work is called 'laid' or 'couched' work. Books bound with this metal ground have always strong work superimposed, usually executed in metal strips, cords, and thread. The silver is now generally oxidised and much darkened, but when new these bindings must have been very brilliant.

The Felbrigge Psalter.   13th-century MS. Probably bound in the 14th century.

The earliest example of an embroidered book in existence is, I believe, the manuscript English Psalter written in the thirteenth century, which afterwards belonged to Anne, daughter of Sir Simon de Felbrigge, K.G., standard-bearer to Richard II. Anne de Felbrigge was a nun in the convent of Minoresses at Bruis-yard in Suffolk, during the latter half of the fourteenth century, and it is quite likely that she herself worked the cover—such work having probably been largely done in monasteries and convents during the middle ages.

On the upper side is a very charming design of the Annunciation, and, on the under, another of the Crucifixion, each measuring $7\frac{3}{4}$ by $5\frac{3}{4}$ inches. In both cases the ground is worked with fine gold threads 'couched' in a zigzag pattern, the rest of

the work being very finely executed in split-stitch
by the use of which apparently continuous lines
can be made, each successive stitch beginning a
little *within* that immediately preceding it—the
effect in some places being that of a very fine
chain-stitch. The lines of this work do not in
any way follow the meshes of the linen or canvas,
as is mostly the case with book-work upon such
material, but they curve freely according to the
lines and folds of the design. It will be recognised I think by art workwomen skilled in
this kind of small embroidery, that the methods
used for ornamenting the canvas binding of this
book are the most artistic of any of the various
means employed for a similar purpose, and I
know of no other instance which for appropriateness of workmanship, or charm of design, can
compare with this, the earliest of all.

The figure of the Virgin Mary, on the upper
side, is dressed in a pale red robe, with an upper
garment or cloak of blue with a gold border. On
her head is a white head-dress, and round it a
yellow halo; just above is a white dove flying
downwards, its head having a small red nimbus
or cloud round it. The Virgin holds a red book
in her hand. The figure of the angel is winged,
and wears an under robe of blue with an upper
garment of yellow; round his head he has a green
and yellow nimbus, his wings are crimson and
white.

Between these two figures is a large yellow
vase, banded with blue and red ; out of it grows a
tall lily, with a crown of three red blossoms.

The drawing of both of the figures is good,
the attitudes and the management of the folds of
the drapery being excellently rendered, and the
execution of the technical part is in no way
inferior to the design.

On the lower side, on a groundwork of gold
similar to that on the upper cover, is a design
of the Crucifixion.   Our Saviour wears a red
garment round the loins, and round his head is
a red and yellow nimbus, his feet being crossed
in a manner often seen in illuminations in ancient
manuscripts.

The cross is yellow with a green edge, the
foot widening out into a triple arch, within which
is a small angel kneeling in the attitude of
prayer.   On the right of the cross is a figure
of the Virgin Mary, in robes of pale blue and
yellow, with a white head-dress and green and
yellow nimbus.   On the left is another figure,
probably representing St. John, dressed in robes
of red and blue, and having a nimbus round his
head of concentric rings of red and yellow.   This
figure is unfortunately in very bad condition.
The edges of the leaves of the book are painted
with heraldic bearings in diamond-shaped spaces,
that of the Felbrigge family 'Gules, a lion
rampant, or' alternately with another 'azure, a

fleur-de-lys, or.' The embroidered sides have
been badly damaged by time and probably more
so by repair. The book has been rebound in
leather, the old embroidered back quite done
away with, and the worked sides pulled away
from their original boards and ruinously flattened
out on the new ones. After the Felbrigge Psalter
no other embroidered binding has been preserved
till we come to one dating about 1536, which is
in satin, and will be described under that head.

The Miroir or Glasse of the Synneful Soul.
MS. by the Princess Elizabeth.   1544.

The Princess Elizabeth, afterwards Queen, in
her eleventh year, copied out in her own hand-
writing the *Miroir or Glasse of the Synneful Soul.*
She says it is translated 'out of frenche ryme into
english prose, joyning the sentences together as
well as the capacitie of my symple witte and
small lerning coulde extende themselves.' It is
also most prettily dedicated: 'From Assherige, the
last daye of the yeare of our Lord God 1544 . . .
To our most noble and vertuous Quene Katherin,
Elizabeth her humble daughter wisheth perpetuall
felicitie and everlasting joye.'

The book is now one of the great treasures
of the Bodleian Library; it is bound in canvas,
measures about 7 by 5 inches, and was embroidered
in all probability by the hands of the Princess

4 The Miroir or Glasse of the Synneful Soul.
MS. by the Princess Elizabeth. 1544.

5—Prayers of Queen Katherine Parr.
MS. by the Princess Elizabeth. 1545.

herself. The Countess of Wilton in her book on the art of needlework says that 'Elizabeth was an accomplished needlewoman,' and that 'in her time embroidery was much thought of.' The Rev. W. Dunn Macray in his *Annals of the Bodleian Library* considers this binding to be one of ' Elizabeth's bibliopegic achievements.'

The design is the same upon both sides. The ground is all worked over in a large kind of tapestry-stitch in thick pale blue silk, very evenly and well done, so well that it has been considered more than once to be a piece of woven material. On this is a cleverly designed interlacing scroll-work of gold and silver braid, in the centre of which are the joined initials K.P.

In each corner is a heartsease worked in thick coloured silks, purple and yellow, interwoven with fine gold threads, and a small green leaflet between each of the petals. The back is very much worn, but it probably had small flowers embroidered upon it.

Prayers of Queen Katherine Parr. MS. by the Princess Elizabeth. 1545.

Another manuscript beautifully written by the Princess Elizabeth about a year later is now at the British Museum. It is on vellum, and contains prayers or meditations, composed originally by Queen Katherine Parr in English, and trans-

E

lated by the Princess into Latin, French, and Italian. The title as given in the book reads, ' Precationes . . . ex piis scriptoribus per nobiliss. et pientiss. D. Catharinam Anglie, Francie, Hibernieq. reginam collecte, et per D. Eliza-betam ex anglico converse.' It is, moreover, dedicated to Henry VIII., the wording being, ' Illustrissimo Henrico octavo, Anglie, Francie, Hibernieq. regi,' etc., and dated Hertford, 20th December 1545.

It is bound in canvas, and measures $5\frac{3}{4}$ by 4 inches, the groundwork being broadly worked in tapestry-stitch, or some stitch analogous to it, in red silk, resembling in method the work on the ground of *The Miroir of the Synneful Soul* already described. On this, in the centre of each side, is a large monogram worked in blue silk, interwoven with silver thread, containing the letters K, probably standing for Katherine, A, F, H, and R, possibly meaning ' Anglie, Francie, Hibernieque, Reginæ,' but like most monograms this one can doubtless be otherwise interpreted. Above and below the monogram are smaller H's, worked in red silk, interwoven with gold thread. In each corner is a heartsease of yellow and purple silk, interwoven with gold thread, and having small green leaves between each of the petals. The work which was once on the back is now so worn that it cannot be traced sufficiently to tell what it originally was. The designs of these two volumes, credited to the Princess Elizabeth, resemble each other to some extent; they both have a monogram in the centre, they both have heartsease in the corners and groundwork of a like character.   They are, as far as workmanship goes, still more alike, similar thick silk is used for the ground, and threads and braids of a thick nature, with metal interwoven, are used on both for the ornamental work.   Speaking of this British Museum book, the Countess of Wilton says, 'there is little doubt that Elizabeth's own needle wrought the ornaments thereon.'

Books embroidered by the Princess Elizabeth.

It cannot be said that there is any actual authority for saying that the two covers just described are really the work of Elizabeth's own hand, although she is known to have been fond of embroidery, it being recorded that she made and embroidered a shirt for her brother Edward when she was six. There is little doubt, however, that the same designer and the same workwoman worked both these covers, and the technique, as well as the design, are peculiar for the time in which they were done. Canvas bindings were rare—most of the embroidered work on books of that period were splendid works on velvet—so that if these two manuscripts had been 'given out' to be bound in embroidered covers we should have expected to find them in rich velvet, like Brion's *Holy Land*, or Christopherson's *Historia Ecclesiastica*, instead of a very elementary braid work. Without attaching too much importance to the various statements concerning their royal origin, I am inclined to think that there is no impossibility, or even improbability, in the supposition that the Princess designed and worked them herself, thereby adding to her exquisite manuscript the further charm of her clever needle. The idea of both writing and embroidering such valued presents as these two books must have been is likely to have strongly appealed to an affectionate and humble daughter, and there is an artistic completeness in the idea which, I think, tells strongly in its favour.

Probably enough no proof of their having been worked by Elizabeth will now ever be forthcoming, but it is equally unlikely that any positive disproof will be found.

The two 'Elizabeth' books stand alone—there are no others resembling them; but the next kind of embroidered work I shall describe is one which includes a large number of books, generally small in size, and usually copies of the Bible or the Psalms. The canvas in these cases is embroidered all over in small tapestry-stitch, the design being shown by means of the different colours of the silks used. The work being all flat it is very strong, and often books bound in this way are

o—Christian Prayers.   London, 1581.

in a marvellous state of preservation. The most
interesting designs are those which represent
Scriptural scenes. Some of these are very curious
and almost grotesque, but there is much excuse
for this. To work a face any way in embroidery
is troublesome enough, but to work it on a small
scale in tent-stitch is especially difficult, the result
being somewhat similar in effect to that of a glass
or marble mosaic, each little stitch being nearly
square and of an uniform colour. The designers
of these embroideries do not appear to have had
a very fertile imagination, as again and again the
same subject is represented. Perhaps the most
favourite of all is Jacob wrestling with the angel ;
of figure subjects 'Faith and Hope' are the
most frequently met with, but 'Peace and Plenty'
are also common enough.

Christian Prayers.   London, 1581.

A *Book of Christian Prayers* with illustrated
borders, printed in London in 1581, is bound in
coarse canvas worked in tapestry-stitch in colours,
and measures 7 by 5 inches. The same design is
on each side — a kind of flower-basket in two
stories, out of the lower part of which, rectangular
in shape, grow two branches, one with lilies and
another with white flowers, and out of the upper,
oval in shape, rise two sprays of roses, one white
the other red.

In the lower corners are a large lily, a blue flower, and a large double-rose spray. All the design is outlined with silver cord or thread, and the veinings of the leaves are indicated in the same way. There are remains of two green velvet ties on the front edges of each of the boards. The back is not divided into panels, but has a design upon it of the letters E and S repeated five times. The edges are gilt and gauffred.

Psalms and Common Praier.   London, 1606-7.

During the seventeenth century little 'double' books were rather favourite forms for Common Prayer and Psalms especially. These curious bindings open opposite ways and have two backs, two ornamental boards, and one unornamented board enclosed between the two books, which are always of the same size.

There are several instances where embroidered books have been bound in this way, the earliest I know being a copy of the Psalms and Common Prayer, printed in 1606-7.

This is bound in canvas, and measures $3\frac{1}{4}$ by 2 inches, each side having the same design embroidered on each of the ornamented sides and backs. The flowers and leaves are worked in long straight stitches in coloured silks, outlined with silver twist. A large pansy plant occupies the place of honour, growing out of a

7—Psalms and Common Praier.   London, 1606.

8—Bible, etc. London, 1612.

small green mound, from which also spring two short plants with five-petalled yellow flowers. The main stems and ribs of the leaves are made with strong silver twist. Round about the central spray are several coloured buds. On the backs are four panels, each containing a small four-petalled flower. The ground is worked all over with silver thread irregularly stitched, and the edges are bound with a broad silver thread. There was originally one ribbon to twist round both books and keep them together, but it is now quite gone. The edges are gilt, gauffred, and slightly coloured.

Bible, etc.   London, 1612.

A copy of the Bible, with the Psalms, printed in London in 1612, and measuring $6\frac{3}{4}$ by $4\frac{1}{4}$ inches, is bound in fine canvas, and bears upon it designs embroidered in coloured silks in tapestry-stitch.

On the upper side is King Solomon seated in an elaborate throne on a dais, all outlined with gold cord. He wears a golden crown and a dress which more nearly approaches the style worn at the date of the production of the book than that which was probably worn by Solomon himself. Before the King kneels a figure, no doubt intended for the Queen of Sheba, in a red and orange robe of a curious fashion. She holds out two white and red roses to the King, who bends to take them. The ground is patterned in green and blue diamonds. The distant landscape shows a castle with turrets, trees, a tower, a house, and a sun with rays. The groundwork on both sides and the back is worked in silver thread.

The lower side has in the centre Jacob wrestling with the angel. Jacob has a beard and a blue cloak; his staff lies on the ground. The angel wears a red flowing robe, and his wings are many-coloured, and enriched with various threads and spirals of gold. The landscape is elaborate. In the foreground is a river with a bridge of planks, a gabled cottage, hospitably smoking from its chimneys, a red lily, and a tree. In the middle distance is a castle with tower and flag, and on the horizon are a windmill, a castle with two towers, and some trees, above all a red cloud. The back is divided into six panels, on each of which is a different design in coloured silks. These designs are small, and although they are in perfectly good condition, the subjects represented are doubtful. The upper and lower panels seem to represent only castles with towers. Then apparently come Jonah and the whale, the creation, the temple, and the deluge with the ark, but it is quite possible that other interpretations might be made. There are remains of two red silk ties on the front edges of each board, and the edges of the leaves are gilded simply.

9.—Sermons by Samuel Ward.   London, 1626-7.

Sermons by Samuel Ward. London, 1626-7.

Mr. Yates Thompson has kindly allowed me to describe and illustrate an embroidered book belonging to him, bound in canvas, and measuring 5¾ by 4¼ inches. It is a collection of sermons preached by 'Samuel Ward, Bachelour of Divinity,' and printed in London, 1626-7, the binding being probably of about the latter date. On the upper cover is a lady in a blue dress, seated, and holding a hawk on her left wrist, and a branch with apples in her right. Round her are scattered flower sprays, honeysuckle, foxglove, a stalk with two large pears, a cluster of grapes, a twig with a butterfly upon it, and a wild-rose spray. The lady, the petals of the flowers, and the leaves are all worked in tapestry-stitch; the bird and the lady's hair in long straight stitches; the stalks, fruits, and grasses are worked in variously coloured silk threads, thickly and strongly bound round with very fine silver wire. The lady has a coif, cuff, and belt of short pieces of silver and gold guimp arranged like a plait.

The under side shows a seated lady in a green dress, playing a lute left-handed. This most unusual position is probably not really intentional, but the drawing has accidentally been reversed. She is surrounded, like her companion with the hawk, by flower sprays, a thistle, cornflower, strawberries, a rose, lily, bluebell, and small

F

bunch of grapes, making a kind of arbour, with a wreath of red cloud at the top. The lady, the petals of the flowers, and the leaves are worked in fine tapestry-stitch; the stalks and fruits in coloured silks, mixed with silver wire. The lady has a coif and a cuff of silver guimp arranged in the same way as that on the other side.

The back is divided into four panels by silver guimp, each containing a flower worked in tapestry-stitch, a blue flower, a wild rose, a pansy, and a thistle. The ground of the whole is loosely overcast with silver thread, the constructive lines of the book being marked by rows of silver guimp arranged in small arches. The edges are bound by a strong silver braid. The head and tail bands are worked in silver thread—an unusual method—and the edges are gilt and gauffred.

There are two ties on each board of striped silk, much frayed and worn, but the embroidered work itself is in excellent condition, and very strong.

New Testament, etc. London, 1625-35.

A small copy of the New Testament, printed in London in 1625, bound together with the Psalms, 1635, is covered with canvas, all worked in tapestry-stitch, and measures 4¼ by 3 inches.

On the upper cover is a full-length figure of Hope, with dark hair, dressed in a red dress with large falling collar, having a blue flower at the

10—New Testament, etc.   London, 1625-35.

point.   In her left hand she holds an anchor.   In
the distant background is a cottage and a gibbet
on a hill, the sun with rays just appearing under
a cloud.   On the hilly foreground is a red lily,
and further afield a caterpillar and a strawberry
plant.   On the lower cover is a full-length figure
of Faith, with fair hair, dressed in a blue dress
with large falling collar, having a red flower at
the point.   In her left hand she holds an open
book with the word 'FAITH' written across it.
On the hilly foreground is a large red tulip and a
plant with red blooms, further afield are ·a pear-
tree and two caterpillars.

On the back are four panels, containing respectively a bird, a blue flower, a squirrel, and a
red flower.

On the front edge of the upper cover can be
seen the remains of one tie of green silk, and the
edges are protected all round by a piece of green
silk braid.   The edges of the leaves are plainly gilt.

This cover is one of the rare instances of a
book bound in embroidered work not made for it,
the embroidery being clearly made for a book of
about half the present thickness.   It is possible
that it was intended for either the New Testament
or the Psalms separately, and, as an after-thought,
was made to do double duty.   But as it now is,
the worked back is just a strip down the middle
of the back itself, the designs of the sides en-
croaching considerably inwards.

The Daily Exercise of a Christian.
London, 1623.

The Daily Exercise of a Christian, printed in London in 1623, and measuring 4¾ by 2¾ inches, is ornamented with a single flower spray, with buds and leaves. The flower is a double rose with curving stem, one large half-opened bud and one smaller, and a few leaves, all worked in tent-stitch. The spray rises from a small bed of grass, out of which grows a small blue flower. In the upper right-hand corner is a small blue cloud. The same design is on both sides. The back is divided into four panels, the divisions being marked and bounded by a thick silver braid, which is also used as an edging all round the book; the designs, beginning at the top, are a fly and a flower alternately, differently coloured.

The background is all worked in with silver thread in chain-stitch. With this book is one of the now rare ornamental markers, which, no doubt, often went with embroidered books. It is fastened to an ornamental oblong cushion, probably made of light wood, and is worked in silver thread and coloured silks in the same manner as the rest of the embroidered work, and finished off at the ends with small red tassels.

11—The Daily Exercise of a Christian.
London, 1623.

12 — Bible   London. 1626.

Bible. London, 1626-28.

A copy of the Bible, printed in London in 1626, is bound in canvas, and measures 6 by 3½ inches.

The embroidery is in coloured silks, silver cords and threads, and silver guimp. On the upper cover is a small full-length figure of St. Peter, with short beard, holding a key in his left hand. He is dressed in a blue under-garment, with red and orange robe over it, all the edges being marked by a silver twist, some of which has come off. The ground is green and in hillocks. All this work is done in coloured silks and silver threads in shading stitch.

On the under side is a figure of St. Paul, with long beard, holding a silver sword in his right hand. He wears a blue under-garment, with red and orange upper robe, all edged with silver twist. The feet of both figures are bare. The rest of the design is the same on both sides. The skies are worked in large stitches of blue and yellow silk and silver threads, graduating from dark to light; above these are canopies of silver thread, couched, and vandyked at the edge. Enclosing the figures are arches with columns, in high relief in silver cords and threads. The inner edge of the arch is curiously marked by a line of brown silk worked over a strip of vellum in the manner used for hand-worked head-bands, and the outer edge has 'crockets' of silver guimp.

The columns rest upon 'rams-horn' curves, heavily worked in relief with silver threads, the insides of the curves worked in brown silk over vellum like the inner edge of the arch.

Metal Threads used on Embroidered Books.

Guimp and gold threads are largely used, as has already been noticed, in embroidered books from early times, but on the next specimen of a canvas-bound book I have chosen for description, dated 1642, a kind of metal thread occurs which is very curious. It is used at an earlier date on satin books, and it is also found more commonly upon them; but as I have put the canvas books first for the purpose of description, and the 'thread' occurs in one of them, this is the best place to put its description. This thread I call 'Purl,' and a thread with this name is mentioned in several places as having been used in England in the seventeenth century; but there is no description of it, so that this thread may not be the 'purl' mentioned by the seventeenth-century writers, but if it is not, I do not know what purl is, neither do I know any other special name for the thread. In order that there may be no doubt as to what I mean by purl, I will shortly describe the thread as I know it.

First there is a very fine copper wire; this is

closely bound round with coloured silk, also very
fine, and in this state it looks simply like a
coloured thread. Then this coloured thread is
itself closely coiled round something like a fine
knitting-needle—in fact I have made it on one—
and then pushed off in the form of a fine coiled
tube. The thread is always cut into short lengths
for use, and on books these short lengths are
generally threaded and drawn together at their
ends, making, so to speak, little arches—so that
although on the under side of the material there
is only a tiny thread, on the upper side there is a
strong arch, practically of copper. On boxes and
other ornamental productions of this same period,
pieces of purl are not infrequently found laid flat
like little bricks; and houses, castles, etc., are
often represented by means of it; but on books
the general use is either for flowers, grounds, or
(in very small pieces) to keep on spangles. Ob-
viously any coloured silk can be used in making
this thread, so that it may be said that for
coloured silk work, where strength is required,
flowers worked in purl are the best. The colours
used when roses are represented are usually
graduated,—yellow or white in the centre, then
gradually darkening outward, yellow, pale pink,
and red, or pale yellow, pale blue, and dark blue.
Purl flowers are usually accessories to some
regular design, but, in one instance at least, to
be described later on, it supplies the entire decoration of a small satin book.

Bible, etc. London, 1642.

The design on a Bible with Psalms, printed
in London in 1642, bound in fine canvas, and
measuring 6 by 3½ inches, is the same on both
sides. The ground is all laid, or couched, with
silver threads, caught down at intervals by small
white stitches. In the centre is a circular silver
boss, and out of this grow four lilies worked
with silver thread in button-hole stitch; each
of these lilies has a shape similar to its own
underneath it, outlined with fine gold cord, and
filled in with red silk; representing altogether
white flowers with a red lining. These four red
and white lilies make together the form of a
Maltese cross, and between each of the arms is a
purl rose with yellow centre and graduated blue
petals. A double oval, with the upper and lower
curves larger than the side ones, marked with a
thick gold cord, encloses the central cross, and
the remaining spaces are filled with ovals and
lines of gold guimp, with here and there a little
patch of red or yellow purl, the extremities of the
upper and lower ovals being filled with threads
of green silk loosely bound with a silver spiral,
worked to represent a green plot.

The upper and lower curves of the oval are
thickened by an arch of gold thread laid length-
wise, and kept in place by little radiating lines of
red silk. In each corner is a purl rose, with

13.—Bible, etc.   London, 1642.

14—Bible. London, 1648.

blue centre, the petals graduating in colour from pale yellow to dark red, with leaf forms and stalks of gold cord and guimp. At the top and bottom of the oval is a many-coloured purl rose, and the spaces still left vacant are dotted with little pieces of red, blue, and yellow purl and spangles. On the front edges are the remains of two red silk ties.

The back is divided into four panels by a thick gold twist. The upper and lower panels have each a blue purl rose worked in them, with a white and red lily in the same silver thread as those on the sides, with gold leaves and stalks; the two inner panels contain each three purl roses, with gold leaves and stems. The upper of these panels has a large rose of blue, yellow, and red, and two smaller ones yellow with blue centres; the lower panel has a large rose of red, pink, and yellow, and two smaller ones of red, with yellow centres.

Dotted about the groundwork of the panels are several spangles and short lengths of coloured purl.

The edges of the leaves are plainly gilt.

Bible. London, 1648.

A Bible, printed in London in 1648, formerly the property of George III., is bound in canvas, and has embroidered upon the boards emblematic representations of Faith and Hope. It measures 6¾ by 4¾ inches.

On the upper side is a full-length figure of Faith. She has fair hair, and is dressed in an orange and red dress cut low, and showing in the front a pale blue under garment. She has a large white collar and cuffs, both in point-lace, and bears in her right hand an open book with the word 'FAITH' written upon it, while her left hand rests upon a pointed shield, pale purple with a yellow centre. She is standing upon a rounded hillock, on which are a strawberry plant with two fruits, two caterpillars, a red tulip, and another flower.

In the right-hand upper corner is a turreted and gabled house, the windows of which are marked with little glittering pieces of talc. Below the house is a caterpillar and a large blue butterfly. In the left-hand upper corner is the sun, in gold, just appearing under a blue cloud. Underneath this, in succession, come a tree with a butterfly upon it, a bird, most likely meant for a wren, and another caterpillar. The remains of two red tie-ribbons are near the front edges. The background is worked in silver thread, and the edges of the boards are bound with silver braid having a thread or two of red silk on the innermost side.

On the under cover Hope appears in a curiously worked upper garment of blue and white,

short in the sleeves, in needlepoint, with a belt.
Under this is a dress of red and orange, showing
a blue under skirt in front.   A scarf of the same
colour as the dress is gracefully folded over the
shoulders and hangs over the left arm ; a rather
deep collar and cuffs are both worked in needlepoint.   The right hand rests upon an anchor
with a ' fouled ' rope.

Hope stands upon a rounded hillock, on which
are a snail and spray of possible foxglove, and
out of which grow a red carnation and another
flower.   In the upper right-hand corner is a
gabled cottage with a tree, and under it a moth,
flower, and caterpillar.   Towards the upper left-
hand corner is a bank of cloud with red and
yellow rays issuing therefrom, and under it a
pear-tree with flower and fruit, and a many-
coloured butterfly.   All the background is worked
in silver thread.

The five panels of the back, indicated with
silver cord, are each filled with a different design.
Beginning at the top, these are : a rose, a parrot
with a red fruit, a double rose, a lion, and a lily.
The edges are plainly gilt.

CHAPTER III

BOOKS BOUND IN VELVET

IT seems probable that velvet was a favourite covering for royal books in England from an early period. Such volumes as remain 'covered in vellat' that belonged to Henry VII. are, however, not embroidered, the ornamentation upon them being worked metal, or enamels upon metal. It is not until the time of Henry VIII. that we have any instances remaining of books bound in embroidered velvet.

Velvet is very troublesome to work upon, the pile preventing any delicate embroidery being done directly upon it, hence the prevalence of gold cords and appliqué work on canvas or linen, on which of course the embroidery may be executed as delicately as may be desired.

Tres ample description de toute la terre Saincte, etc. [By Martin de Brion.] MS. of the sixteenth century, probably bound about 1540.

The earliest extant English binding in embroidered velvet covers this manuscript, which

15—Tres ample description de toute la terre Saincte, etc.
MS.   1540.

belonged to Henry VIII., and is dedicated to him. The manuscript is on vellum, and is beautifully illuminated. It is bound in rich purple velvet, and each side, measuring 9 by 6 inches, is ornamented with the same design. In the centre is a large royal coat-of-arms, surrounded by the garter, and ensigned with a royal crown. The coat-of-arms and the garter are first worked in thick silks of the proper colours, red and blue, laid or couched, with small stitches of silk of the same colour, arranged so as to make a diamond pattern, on fine linen or canvas. On the coat are the arms of France and England quarterly; the bearings, respectively three fleur-de-lys and three lions, are solidly worked in gold cord, and the whole is appliqué on to the velvet with strong stitches. On the blue garter the legend 'Honi soit qui mal y pense' is outlined in gold cord, between each word being a small red rose, the buckle, end, and edge of the garter being marked also in gold cord, and the whole appliqué like the coat. The very decorative royal crown is solidly worked in gold cords of varying thickness directly on to the velvet. The rim or circlet has five square jewels of red and blue silk along it, between each of these being two seed pearls. From the rim rise four crosses-patée and four fleurs-de-lys, at the base of each of which is a pearl, and also one in each inner corner of the crosses-patée. Four arches also rise from the rim, the two outer ones each having three small scrolls with a pearl in the middle; at the top is a mound and cross-patée, with a pearl in each of its inner corners. There is a letter H on each side of the coat-of-arms, and these letters were originally doubtless worked with seed pearls, but the outlines of them alone are now left. In each corner is a red Lancastrian rose worked on a piece of satin, appliqué, the centres and petals marked in gold cord, and the whole enclosed in an outer double border of gold cord. On the front edges of each side are the remains of two red silk ties.

This is certainly a very handsome piece of work, and is wonderfully preserved. It is the earliest example of a really fine embroidered book on velvet in existence, and it has perhaps been more noticed and illustrated than any other book of its kind. The crown has an interesting peculiarity about it, which does not appear, as far as I have observed, on any other representation of it, namely, that the four arches take their rise directly from the rim. They generally rise from the summits of the crosses-patée, but I should fancy that the rise from the circlet itself is more correct.

Biblia. Tiguri, 1543.

This Bible also belonged to Henry viii. It is bound in velvet, originally some shade of red or crimson, but now much faded. It measures 15

16   Biblia.   Tiguri, 1543.

17— Il Petrarcha. Venetia. 1544.

by 9¼ inches. It is ornamented with arabesques and initials all outlined with fine gold cord. In the centre are the initials H. R., bound together by an interlacing knot, within a circle. Arabesques above and below the circle make up an inner panel, itself enclosed by a broad border of arabesques, with a double, or Tudor, rose in each corner. The edges of the leaves of the book are elaborately painted with heraldic designs.

It has been re-backed with leather, but still retains the original boards.

Il Petrarcha.   Venetia, 1544.

Another fine example of the decorative use of Heraldry occurs on a copy of Petrarch printed at Venice in 1544, and probably bound about 1548, after the death of Henry VIII. It belonged to Queen Katherine Parr, and bears her arms with several quarterings—worked appliqué on rich blue purple velvet, and measures 7 by 6 inches. The first coat is the 'coat of augmentation' granted to the Queen by Henry VIII.—'Argent, on a pile gules, between six roses of the same, three others of the field'—and the next coat is that of 'Parr.'

The various quarterings on this coat are worked differently from those on the last book described. Here the red and blue are well shown by pieces of coloured satin—except in the first, fifth, and seventh coats, where there is some couched work in diamond pattern, just like that on Martin Brion's book. The entire coat, which is of an ornamental shape, is appliqué in one large piece, and edged by a gold cord. The crown surmounting it is heavily worked in gold guimp—the cap being represented in crimson silk thread and all appliqué. There are two supporters—that on the right, an animal breathing flame, and gorged with a coronet from which hangs a long chain, all worked in coloured silks on linen and appliqué, belongs to the Fitzhugh family, the coat of which is shown on the third quarter; that on the left, a wyvern argent, also gorged with a coronet, from which depends a long gold chain, is that of the Parr family. The wyvern is a piece of blue silk, finished in gold and silver cords, in appliqué. The gold cord enclosing the armorial design is amplified at each corner into an arabesque scroll. The book has been most unfortunately rebound, and the work is badly strained in consequence—the back being entirely new; nevertheless it is in a wonderful state of preservation. It is said to have been worked by Queen Katherine Parr herself. The design is too large for the book, and the crown is too large for the coat-of-arms. It is probable that the binding of the book was done after the death of Henry VIII., otherwise the supporters would have been the lion and the greyhound; also the

18—Queen Mary's Psalter. 14th-century MS.

coat-of-arms would have been different; also, as
the Seymour coat does not appear, it is likely
that the binding was done before Queen Katherine
Parr's marriage with Lord Seymour of Sudley,
in 1547.   The design is the same on both sides.

Queen Mary's Psalter.   14th-century MS.
Bound about 1553.

The beautiful English manuscript of the
fourteenth century known as 'Queen Mary's
Psalter' was presented to her in 1553.   It is
bound in crimson velvet, measuring 11 by $6\frac{3}{4}$
inches, and appliqué on each side is a large conventional pomegranate-flower worked on fine
linen in coloured silks and gold thread.   This
flower is much worn, but enough is left to show
that it was originally finely worked.   Queen
Mary used the pomegranate as a badge in
memory of her mother, Katharine of Aragon.
The volume has been re-backed in plain crimson
velvet, and still retains the original gilt corners
with bosses, and two clasps, on the plates of which
are engraved the Tudor emblems,—portcullis,
dragon, lion, and fleur-de-lys.

Christopherson, *Historia Ecclesiastica*.
Lovanii, 1569.

Many fine bindings in embroidered velvet of
the time of Queen Elizabeth still remain, several
of them having been her own property.

H

One of the most decorative of these last is unfortunately in a very bad state, owing possibly to the fact that there were originally very many separate pearls upon it, and that these have from time to time been wilfully picked off. The book is in three volumes, and is a copy of the *Historia Ecclesiastica*, written by Christopherson, Bishop of Chichester, and printed at Louvain in 1569. Each of these volumes is bound in the same way, so the description of one of them will serve for all, except that no one volume is perfect, so the description must be taken as representing only what each originally was.

It is covered in deep green velvet, and measures 6 by 3½ inches, the design being the same on each side. In the centre the royal coat-of-arms is appliqué in blue and red satin, on an ornamental cartouche of pink satin, with scrolls of gold threads and coloured silks, richly dotted with small pearls. The bearings on the coats-of-arms are solidly worked in fine gold threads.

From each corner of the sides springs a rose spray, with Tudor roses of red silk mixed with pearls, and Yorkist roses all worked in pearls clustering tight together, the leaves and stems being made in gold cord and guimp. A decoratively arranged ribbon outlined with gold cord and filled in with a line of small pearls set near each other, encloses the design, and numerous

20 Christian Prayers. London, 1570.

single pearls are set in the spaces between the roses and their leaves and stems.

The back is divided into five panels bearing alternately Yorkist roses of pearls and Tudor roses of red silk and pearls, all worked in the same way as the roses on the sides.

The illustration I give of this binding (Frontispiece) is necessarily a restoration. But there is nothing added which was not originally on the book. Each pearl that has disappeared has left a little impress on the velvet, and so has each piece of gold cord which has been pulled off. The back is still existing; but bad though both sides and back now are, it is much better they should be in their present condition than that they should have been mended or replaced in parts by newer material.

Christian Prayers.   London, 1570.

A simpler binding, but still one of great richness, covers a copy of *Christian Prayers*, printed in London in 1570.

This is covered in crimson velvet, measuring 6 by 3½ inches, and is worked largely with metal threads, mixed with coloured silks. In the centre is the crest of the family of Vaughan—a man's head with a snake round the neck. The crest rests on a fillet, and is enclosed in a twisted circle of gold with four coloured bosses. From the upper and lower extremities of this circle spring two flower forms in gold and silver guimp, with sprays issuing from them bearing strawberries, grape bunches, and leaves, in the upper half, and roses and leaves in the lower. The grapes are represented by rather large spangles, and the leaves, worked in gold, have a few strands of green silk in them ; large spangles, kept down by a short piece of guimp, are used to fill in spaces here and there. This is the first instance of the use of spangles on a velvet book. The back is tastefully ornamented with gold cord arranged diamond-wise, and having in each diamond a flower worked in gold.

Parker, *De antiquitate Ecclesiæ Britannicæ.* London, 1572.

This is one of the embroidered books that belonged to Queen Elizabeth, and has been frequently illustrated and described. It is remarkable in other respects than for its binding, as it is one of a number of probably not more than twenty copies of a work by Matthew Parker, Archbishop of Canterbury, *De antiquitate Ecclesiæ Britannicæ*, printed for him by John Day in London, 1572. It was the first instance of a privately printed book being issued in England.

Archbishop Parker had a private press, and

21.—Parker, De antiquitate Ecclesiæ Britannicæ.
London, 1572.

his books were printed with types cast at his own
cost, John Day being sometimes employed as his
workman.   No two copies of this particular work
are alike, and it is supposed that the Archbishop
continually altered the sheets as they came from
the press and had the changes effected at once.
The book has two title-pages, each of which, as
well as a leaf containing the arms of the Bishops
in vellum, the ornamental borders, and coats-of-
arms throughout the book, are emblazoned in gold
and colours.

The biographies of sixty-nine Archbishops
are contained in the book, but not Parker's
own.   This omission was supplied afterwards
by a little satirical tract published in 1574,
entitled 'Histriola, a little storye of the actes
and life of Matthew, now archbishop of Canterbury.'

But the Archbishop not only had his printing
done under his own roof, but also had in his
house 'Paynters . . . wryters, and Boke-binders,'
so that it may fairly enough be considered that he
bound the splendid copy of his great work which
was intended for the Queen's acceptance, in a
specially handsome manner, under his own
direct supervision, and in accordance not only
with his own taste but also with that of his
royal mistress.   The volume is a large one,
measuring 10 by 7 inches, and is covered in dark
green velvet.   On both sides the design is a rebus

on the name of Parker, representing in fact a Park within a high paling. The palings are represented as if lying flat, and are worked in gold cord with flat strips of silver, on yellow satin appliqué. There are gates and other small openings in the continuity of the line of palings. On the upper cover within the paling is a large rose-bush, bearing a large Tudor rose and two white roses in full bloom, with buds and leaves, some tendrils extending over the palings. The stalks are of silver twist edged with gold cord, the red flowers are worked with red silk and gold cord, the white ones made up with small strips of flat silver and gold cord. Detached flowers and tufts of grass grow about the rose-tree; among these are two purple and yellow pansies, Elizabeth's favourite flowers, and in each corner is a deer, one 'courant,' one 'passant,' one feeding, and one 'lodged.'

The design fills the side of the book very fully, and the workmanship is everywhere excellent. This upper cover is much faded, as it has been for many years exposed to the light in one of the Binding show-cases in the King's Library at the British Museum.

The under side is much fresher, but the design not so elaborate. There is a similar paling to that on the other side, the 'Park' being dotted about with several plants, ferns, and tufts of grass. Near each corner is a deer, one feeding,

22—The Epistles of St. Paul.   London, 1578.
(*From a drawing*).

one 'couchant,' one 'tripping,' and one 'courant,' and one 'lodged' in the centre. There are also two snakes worked in silver thread with small colour patches in silk.

The back is badly worn, but the original design can be easily traced upon it. There were five panels, in each of which is a small rose-tree, bearing one large flower, with leaves and buds, and tufts of grass. The first, third, and fifth of these are white Yorkist roses; the second and third are Tudor roses of white and red.

The Epistles of St. Paul.   London, 1578.

If this book of Archbishop Parker's is one of the most elaborately ornamented embroidered books existing, and perhaps one of the greatest treasures of its kind in the British Museum, the next velvet book to describe is one of the simplest, yet it also is one of the greatest treasures of its kind at the Bodleian Library.

It is a small copy of the Epistles of St. Paul, printed by Barker in London, 1578, and measuring 4½ by 3½ inches, and it belonged to Queen Elizabeth. Inside she has written a note in which she says: 'I walke manie times into the pleasant fieldes of the Holy Scriptures, where I plucke up the goodlie greene herbes of sentences by pruning, eate them by reading, chawe them by musing, and laie them up at length in the hie seat of memorie by gathering them together, so that having tasted thy swetenes I may the less perceive the bitterness of this miserable life.'

The Rev. W. D. Macray, in the *Annals of the Bodleian Library*, says, 'This belonged to Queen Elizabeth, and is bound in a covering worked by herself'; and the Countess of Wilton, in the *Art of Embroidery*, says, 'The covering is done in needlework by the Queen herself.'

It is also described by Dibdin in *Bibliomania*. He says, 'The covering is done in needlework by the Queen herself.'

The black velvet binding is much worn, and has been badly repaired. The work upon it is all done in silver cord or guimp, and the designing, as well as the work, is such as may well have been done by the Queen.

On both covers borders with legends in Latin, enclosed in lines of gold cord, run parallel to the edges. Beginning at the right-hand corners of each side, these legends read, ' Beatus qui divitias scripturæ legens verba vertit in opera—Celum Patria Scopus vitæ xpus—Christus via—Christo vive.' In the centre of the upper side is a ribbon outlined in gold cord, with the words, ' Eleva sursum ibi ubi,' a heart being enclosed within the ribbon, and a long stem with a flower at the top passing through it. In the centre of the lower side a similar ribbon with the motto, ' Vicit omnia pertinax virtus,' encloses a daisy, a badge pre-

23—Christian Prayers, etc.　London, 1584.

viously used by Henry VIII. and Edward VI.,
probably in memory of their ancestress, Margaret
Beaufort.   Both these inner scrolls have the
initial letter E interwoven with them.

There is no doubt that the usual royal embroidered bindings of the time of Elizabeth were
elaborately designed and richly worked, in decided
contrast to this small book ; and this difference of
style makes it more probable that the Queen
worked it herself.

There is no resemblance between this book
and the two canvas-bound books already described
which are attributed to her, except the use of cord
alone in the embroidery ; but the difference of
material might perhaps be considered sufficient
to account for this.   No real evidence seems
to be forthcoming as to the authorship of the
embroidered work, but there is no doubt that the
book was a favourite one of Queen Elizabeth's,
and if the needlework had been done for her by
any of the ladies of her Court, it would be likely
that she would have added a note to that effect to
the words she has written inside.

Christian Prayers, etc.   London, 1584.

A copy of *Christian Prayers*, with the Psalms,
printed in London in 1581 and 1584, is curiously
bound in soft paper boards strengthened on the
inner side with pieces of morocco and covered

with pale tawny velvet.   It measures $7\frac{1}{2}$ by $5\frac{1}{2}$ inches.   The edges of the leaves are gilt and gauffred.

The arrangement of the design is unusual.   It starts from the centre of the back in the form of a broad ornamental border, extending towards the front edges along the lines of the boards.   This border is handsomely ornamented by a wavy line of silver cords, filled out with conventional flowers and arabesques worked in gold and silver cords and threads, with a little bit of coloured silk here and there.   A symmetrical design of flower forms and arabesques starts, on each board, from the centre of the inner edge of the border, and is worked in a similar way.   Some of the leaves, however, have veinings marked by strips of flat silver, and others made by a flattened silver spiral, having the appearance of a succession of small rings.   There are the remains of two pale orange silk ties on the front edges of each board, and the edges are gilt and gauffred with a little colour.

The petals of the flowers are worked in guimp, whether gold or silver is difficult to say.   Indeed in many instances of the older books it is difficult to be sure whether a metal cord or thread was originally gilded or not, as all these 'gold' threads are, or were, silver gilt, so that when worn the silver only remains.   If the cord or thread has been protected in any corners, however, or if it

24.- Orationis Dominicæ Explicatio, etc.
Genevæ, 1583.

can be lifted a little, the faint trace of gold can often be seen on what would otherwise have been surely put down as originally silver.

Orationis Dominicæ Explicatio, etc.
Genevæ, 1583.

There is in the British Museum a copy of *Orationis Dominicæ Explicatio, per Lambertum Danæum*, printed at Geneva in 1583, which belonged to Queen Elizabeth. It is bound in black velvet, measures 6¾ by 4¼ inches, and is ornamented most tastefully, each side having an arabesque border in gold cord and silver guimp, enclosing a panel with a design of white and red roses, with stems and leaves worked in gold cord and silver guimp with a trifle of coloured silk on the red roses and on the small leaves showing between the petals. On the front edge are the remains of red and gold ties. The design of this charming little book is excellent, and the colour of it when new must have been very effective. The design is the same on both sides. The back is in bad condition, and is panelled with arabesques in gold and silver cord.

Bible. London, 1583.

The most decorative, and in many ways the finest, of all the remaining embroidered books of the time of Elizabeth is now at the Bodleian Library at Oxford. It is one of the 'Douce' Bibles, printed in London in 1583, and probably bound about the same time. It was the property of the Queen herself, and is bound in crimson velvet, measuring 17 by 12 inches. The design is the same on both sides, and consists of a very cleverly arranged scroll of six rose stems, bearing flowers, buds, and leaves springing from a large central rose, with four auxiliary scrolls crossing the corners and intertwining at their ends. The large rose in the centre as well as those near the corners are Tudor roses, the red shown in red silk and the white in silver guimp, both outlined with gold cord. Small green leaves are shown between each of the outer petals. These flowers are heavily and solidly worked in high relief. The smaller flowers are all of silver, the buds, some red, some white. The stems are of thick silver twist enclosed between finer gold cords, and the leaves show a little green silk among the gold cord with which they are outlined and veined. Immediately above and below the centre rose are two little T's worked in small pearls.

The narrow border round the edges is very pretty; it is a wavy line of gold cord and green silk, the hollows within the curves being filled with alternate 'Pods' with pearls, and green leaves. The back is divided into four panels by wavy lines of gold cord and pearls, and the upper

25—Bible. London, 1583.

26--The Commonplaces of Peter Martyr.
London, 1583.

and lower panels have small rose-plants with
white roses, buds, and leaves; the inner panels have
each a large Tudor rose of red and white, with
leaves and buds.   The drawing and designing
of this splendid book are admirable, and the
workmanship is in every way excellent.   Many of
the pearls are gone, and some of the higher portions of the large roses are abraded, the back, as
usual, being in a rather bad state; but in spite
of all this, and the inevitable fading, the work
remains in a sufficiently preserved condition to
show that at this period the art of book-
embroidery reached its highest decorative point.
It is rather curious to note that Henry viii. used
the red Lancastrian rose by preference, but that
on Elizabeth's books the white rose always appears, and I know of very few instances where
the red rose appears on her books.   Of course
both sovereigns used the combined, double, or
Tudor rose as well.

The Commonplaces of Peter Martyr.
London, 1583.

An embroidered book designed in a manner
which is characteristic of a gold tooled book is
found but rarely.   An instance of this however is
found on a copy of *The Commonplaces of Peter
Martyr*, translated by Anthonie Marten, and
printed in London in 1583.   It is covered in

blue purple velvet measuring 13½ by 9 inches,
and the design upon it is a broad outer border
doubly outlined with a curious and effective braid,
apparently consisting of a close series of small
silver rings, but really being only a silver spiral
flattened out. This border is dotted at regular
intervals with star-shaped clusters of small pieces
of silver guimp symmetrically arranged. The
centre of the inner panel is a diamond-shaped
ornament made with similar 'ring' braid and
small pieces of silver guimp, and the corner-pieces
are quarter circles worked in the same way. This
design of centre-piece and corner-pieces is distinctly borrowed from leather work, and I have
never seen another example of the kind executed
in needlework. The colouring of this book is
very good, the purple and silver harmonising in a
very pleasing manner.

Biblia. Antverpiæ, 1590.

A beautiful binding of green velvet covers a
Bible printed at Antwerp in 1590, measuring
7 by 4 inches. The design is the same on both
sides, and the book was apparently bound for
' T. G.,' whose initials are worked into the design ;
a conventional arrangement of curving stems and
flower forms worked in gold cord, guimp, and
small pearls thickly encrusted ; the same on both
boards. The centre is a large conventional

27. Biblia. Antverpiæ. 1590.

28—Udall, Sermons.   London, 1596.
(From a drawing).

flower, in form resembling a carnation, with serrated petals, having a garnet below it, and flanked by the letters T. G., all thickly worked with reed pearls.   In each corner is a smaller flower—conventionalised forms probably of honey-suckle and rose—joined together by curving stems of gold cord, filled out with leaves and arabesques, all together forming a very decorative panel. The outer border is richly worked with leaves and arabesques in guimp and pearls, the outer line of gold cord being ornamented with small triple points marked with pearls.   The back is divided into three spaces by curving lines of gòld cord, and in each of these spaces is worked one of the same conventionalised flower forms as occur on the boards, *i.e.* a honeysuckle, cornflower, and rose, with leaves and smaller curves of gold cord.

The ground of the entire work is freely orna-mented with gilt spangles held down by small pieces of guimp, and with single pearls; the larger of these are enclosed within circles of guimp, the smaller are simply sewn on one by one.

There are remains of gilt clasps on the front edges of each of the boards, and the edges of the leaves are gilt and gauffred, with a little pale colour.

Udall, *Sermons*.   London, 1596.

A few specimens of embroidered books were exhibited at the Burlington Fine Arts Club in

1891. Among them was a charming velvet binding that belonged to Queen Elizabeth, lent by S. Sandars, Esq., and now in the University Library, Cambridge. It is a copy of Udall's *Sermons*, printed in London in 1596, and is covered in crimson velvet, measuring about 6 by 4 inches. The design is the same on each side, the royal coat-of-arms appliqué, with the initials E. R., and a double rose in each corner with stalks and leaves. The coat-of-arms is made up with pieces of blue and red satin, the bearings heavily worked with gold thread, and the ground also thickly studded with small straight pieces of guimp, doubtless put there to insure the greater flatness of the satin. The crown with which the coat-of-arms is ensigned is all worked in guimp, and is without the usual cap. The ornaments on the rim are only trefoils, and there are five arches.

The initials flanking the coat are worked in guimp, as are the corner roses and leaves. The guimp used is apparently silver, and the cord used for the outlines and stems is gold. The back has a gold line down the middle and along the joints, with a wavy line of gold cord each side of it.

Collection of Sixteenth-Century Tracts.
Bound about 1610.

To Henry, Prince of Wales, we owe a great debt of gratitude, as he was the first person of

29   Collection of Sixteenth-Century Tracts.

much consequence in our royal family to take
any real interest in the Old Royal Library.

Indeed it may be considered that the existence
to-day of the splendid 'Old Royal' Library of
the kings of England, which was presented to
the nation in 1759 by George II., is largely due
to the attention drawn to its interest and value by
Prince Henry, who moreover added considerably
to it himself.

This Prince used as his favourite and personal
badge the beautiful design of three white ostrich
feathers within a golden coronet, and with the
motto 'ICH DIEN' on a blue ribbon. With regard
to the origin of this badge there is unfortunately
a good deal of obscurity. The usual explanation
is that it was the helmet-crest of the blind king
of Bohemia, who was killed at Crécy in 1346,
and that in remembrance of this it was adopted
by the Black Prince as his badge. But, as a
matter of fact, the ostrich feather was used as a
family badge by all the sons of Edward III. and
their descendants. It appears to have been the
cognisance of the province of Ostrevant, a dis-
trict lying between Artois and Hainault, and the
appanage of the eldest sons of the house of Hainault. In this way it may have been adopted by
the family of Edward III. by right of his wife,
Philippa of Hainault.

An early notice of the ostrich feather as a
royal badge occurs in a note in one of the Har-

K

leian MSS. to the effect that 'Henrye, son to the
erle of Derby, fyrst duke of Lancaster, gave the
red rose crowned, whose ancestors gave the fox
tayle in his proper cooler, and the ostrych fether,
the pen ermine,' the Henry here mentioned being
the father of Blanche, wife of John of Gaunt.

On the tomb of Prince Arthur, son of Henry
VII., at Worcester, the feather is shown both
singly and in plume, and it occurs in the triple
plume form within a coronet and a scroll with
the words 'ICH DIEN' upon it, on bindings made
by Thomas Berthelet for Prince Edward, son of
Henry VIII., who never was Prince of Wales.

It really seems as if the first 'Prince of Wales'
actually to use the ostrich feather plumes as a
personal badge of that dignity was Prince Henry,
and it occurs largely on such books belonging
to his library as he had rebound, and also on
books that were specially bound for presentation
to him.

This is the case in one of the most decorative
bindings he possessed, enclosing a collection of
tracts originally the property of Henry VIII., but
which somehow or other became the property of
Magdalen College, Cambridge, the governing
body of which had it bound in embroidered
velvet and presented to Prince Henry.

The cover is of crimson velvet, the edges of
which extend freely beyond the edges of the book,
bound all round with a fringe of gold cord. It

30—Bacon. Opera.   Londini. 1623.

measures about 8 by 6 inches.   The design is the
same on each side.   In the centre is a large triple
plume of ostrich feathers, thickly and beautifully
worked in small pearls, within a golden coronet,
and having below them the motto 'ICH DIEN' in
gold upon a blue silk ribbon.

The badge is enclosed in a rectangular panel
of gold cords, in each corner of which is an
ornamental spray of gold cords, guimp, and a
flower in pearls.   A broad border with a richly
designed arabesque of gold guimp or cord, with
pearl flowers, encloses the central panel.   The
design is filled in freely with small pearls enclosed
in guimp circles and small pearls alone.

The back has an ornamental design in gold
cord and guimp.   This cover is a beautiful
specimen of later decorative work on velvet, and
the general effect is extremely rich, the design
and workmanship being equally well chosen as
regards the materials to which they are applied,
and with which they are worked.

Bacon, *Opera*.   Londini, 1623.

A copy of the works of Francis Bacon, Viscount
St. Albans, printed in London in 1623, is bound
in rich purple velvet, and measures 13¼ by 8¾
inches.   The design is a central panel with
arabesque centre and corners, surrounded by a
deep border of close curves and arabesques, all

worked in gold cord and guimp. There are several gold spangles used, kept down by a small piece of gold guimp. The front edges of each board have only the marks left where two ties originally were, and the edges of the book are simply gilt.

Bacon, *Essays.* 1625.

A copy of another work by the same author, the Essays printed in 1625, was given by him to the Duke of Buckingham, and is now at the Bodleian Library at Oxford. It is bound in dark green velvet, measuring about 7 by 5 inches, the same design being embroidered on each side. In the centre is a small panel portrait of the Duke of Buckingham, with short beard, and wearing the ribbon of the Garter. The portrait is mostly worked with straight perpendicular stitches, except the hair and collar, in which the stitches are differently arranged. The background merges from nearly white just round the head to pink at the outer edge ; the coat is brownish. The framework of the portrait is solidly worked in gold braids and silver guimp in relief, the design being of an architectural character. Two columns, with floral capitals and pediments, spring from a scroll-work base and support what may perhaps be intended for a gothic arch with crockets. Immediately above the crown of the arch is a ducal coronet, and a handsome border of elaborate

31—Bacon, Essays.   1625.

32 —Common Prayer. London, 1638.

arabesques reaching far inwards is worked all
round the edges. The outlines of these arabesques,
the stalks and curves, are all worked in gold
cords, the petals and leaves in silver guimp in
relief. The back is divided into eight panels by
gold and silver cords, and in each of these panels
is a four-petalled flower with small circles. There
are several gilt spangles kept down by a small
piece of guimp.

Common Prayer. London, 1638.

Among the few older royal books in the
library at Windsor Castle is an embroidered one
that belonged to Prince Charles, afterwards
Charles II. It is a copy of the *Book of Common
Prayer*, printed in London in 1638, and is bound
in blue velvet with embroidered work in gold
cord and silver guimp, similar in character to
that on the copy of Bacon's *Essays* just described.
It measures 8 by 6 inches. The design is heraldic.
In the centre is the triple plume of the Prince of
Wales, with coronet and label, no motto being
apparent on the latter. The plume is encircled
by the Garter appliqué, on pale blue silk, the
motto, worked in silver cord, being nearly worn
off. Resting on the top of the Garter is a large
princely coronet, flanking which are the letters
'C. P.' In the lower corners are a thistle and a
rose. A broad border with arabesques encloses

the central panel.   This book was exhibited by
Her Majesty at the Burlington Fine Arts Club
in 1891.   It is in very bad condition, which is
curious, as it is not so very old, and as it is still
among the royal possessions it might well have
been imagined that it would have been better
preserved than other and older books of a like
kind which we know have been considerably
moved about.   The colour is however very
charming still, and books have rarely been bound
in blue velvet, black, green, or crimson being
most usual.

After 1649, or thereabouts, there was a full
stop for a time to any art production in the
matter of bookbinding.   Indeed, for the embroidered books as a class that is the end, but
nevertheless a few examples are found at a later
date, but no regular production and no original
designs.

Bible.   Cambridge, 1674.

A large Bible printed at Cambridge in 1674,
in two volumes, was bound in crimson velvet for
James II., presumably about 1685.   The work
upon it, each volume being the same, is of a
showy character, good and strong, but utterly
wanting in any of the artistic qualities either of
design or execution which characterised so many
of the earlier examples.   In the centre are the
initials 'J. R.' surmounted by a royal crown, heavily

33—Bible. Cambridge, 1674.

worked in gold braid, guimp, and some coloured silks. Enclosing the initials and crown are scrolls in thick gold twist; these again are surrounded by a curving ribbon of gold, intertwined with roses and leafy sprays. In each corner is a silver-faced cherub with beads for eyes and gold wings, and at the top a small blue cloud with sun rays, tears dropping from it. There are two broad silk ties to the front of each board, heavily fringed with gold.

The back is divided into nine panels, each containing an arabesque ornament worked in gold cord and thread, the first and last panels being larger than the others and containing a more elaborate design. The edges of the leaves are simply gilt, and the boards measure 18 by 12 inches each, the largest size of any embroidered book known to me.

CHAPTER IV

BOOKS BOUND IN SATIN

Collection of Sixteenth-Century Tracts.
Bound probably about 1536.

ERHAPS the earliest existing English book bound in satin is a collection of sixteenth-century tracts that belonged to Henry VIII., and is now part of the Old Royal Library in the British Museum. It is covered in red satin, measures 12 by 8 inches, and is embroidered in an arabesque design, outlined with gold cord. On the edges the words 'Rex in aeternum vive Neez' are written in gold. The word 'Neez' or 'Nez,' as it is sometimes spelt, may mean Nebuchadnezzar, as the other words were addressed to him. On books bound in leather by Thomas Berthelet, royal binder to Henry VIII. and his immediate successors, the motto often occurs, and as he is known to have bound books in 'crymosyn satin,' this is most likely his work. The pattern

34   Collection of Sixteenth-Century Tracts.

35—New Testament in Greek.
Leyden, 1570.

is worked irregularly all round the boards, and a
sort of arabesque bridge crosses the centres. The
back is new, and of leather, but the boards themselves are the original ones, and the embroidery
is in a very fair condition.

New Testament in Greek.   Leyden, 1576.

If early bindings in satin are rare, still rarer
is the use of silk.   One example worked on
white ribbed silk still remains that belonged to
Queen Elizabeth.   It measures 4¾ by 2¾ inches,
and in its time was no doubt a very decorative
and interesting piece of work, but it is now in
a very dilapidated state, largely due to improper
repairing.   The book has actually been rebound
in leather, and the old embroidered sides stuck
on.   So it must be remembered that my illustration of it is considerably restored.   The design,
alike on both sides, is all outlined with gold cords
and twists of different kinds and thicknesses, and
the colour is added in water-colours on the silk.
In the centre is the royal coat-of-arms within an
oval garter ensigned with a royal crown, in the
adornment of which a few seed pearls are used,
as they are also on the ends of the garter.

Enclosing the coat-of-arms is an ornamental
border of straight lines and curves, worked with
a thick gold twist, intertwined with graceful
sprays of double and single roses, outlined in

L

gold and coloured red, with buds and leaves. A few symmetrical arabesques, similarly outlined and coloured, fill in some of the remaining spaces. The work on this book, a *New Testament in Greek*, printed at Leyden in 1576, is like no other; but the general idea of the design, rose-sprays cleverly intertwined, is one that may be considered characteristic of the Elizabethan embroidered books, as it frequently occurs on them. The use of water-colour with embroidery is very rare, and it is never found on any but silk or satin bindings, generally as an adjunct in support of coloured-silk work over it, but in this single instance it is used alone.

Seventeenth-Century Embroidered Books.

The books described hitherto have been specimens of rare early instances, but in the seventeenth century there is a very large field to choose from. Small books, mostly religious works, were bound in satin from the beginning of the century until the time of the Commonwealth in considerable numbers; so much so, in fact, that their value depends not so much upon their designs or workmanship as upon their condition.

It is generally considered that embroidered books are extremely delicate, but this is not so; they will stand far more wear than would be imagined from their frail appearance. The embroidered work actually protects the satin, and such signs of wear as are visible are often found rather in the satin itself, where unprotected, than in the work upon it. In many cases a peculiar appearance, which is often mistaken for wear, is seen in the case of representations of insects, caterpillars, or butterflies particularly. These creatures, or parts of them, appear to consist only of slight stitches of plain thread, suggesting either that the work has never been finished, or else that the finished portions have worn away. The real fact is, however, that these places have been originally worked with small bright pieces of peacock's feather, which have either tumbled out or been eaten away by minute insects, a fate to which it is well known peacocks' feathers are particularly liable.

The late Lady Charlotte Schreiber, who was a great collector of pieces of old embroidery, among a host of other curious things possessed the only perfect instance of work of this kind of the seventeenth century I have ever been fortunate enough to find. It was a very realistic caterpillar, closely and completely worked with very small pieces of peacocks' feathers, sewn on with small stitches, quite confirming the opinion I had already formed as to the original filling in of the usual 'bald' spaces representing such objects.

Bible. London, 1619.

A copy of a Bible, printed in London in 1619, is bound in white satin, and measures 6 by 3½ inches. On each side is an emblematic figure enclosed in an oval ; the figures are different, but their surroundings are alike. On the upper side a lady holding a palm branch in her right hand is worked in shading-stitch. She is full length, and wears an orange skirt with purple robe over it confined by a blue belt, and over her shoulders a pink jacket—all these garments are outlined by a gold cord. Her fair hair is covered by an ornamental cap of red and gold, and her feet are bare.

The ground is worked with coloured silks and threads of fine wire closely twisted round with coloured silks, and the sky, painted in gradations of pink in water-colours, is worked sparsely with long stitches of blue silk.

The lower side shows a female figure worked in a similar way ; in this case she bears in her right hand some kind of wand or spray, which has nearly worn off, and in her left a bunch of corn or grapes, or something of that kind which has also badly worn away. If the first figure may be considered to represent Peace, this one may perhaps be Plenty. She wears a deep purplish skirt, with full over-garment and body of the same colour, with an under-jacket of white and gold. On her

36—Bible. London, 1619.

37 Emblemes Chrestiens. MS. 1624.

dark hair she has a blue flower with red leaves. Her feet are bare. The ground and sky are both worked in the same way as the other side. Both figures are enclosed in a flat oval border of gold thread, broad at the top and narrowing towards the foot. In the corners are symmetrical arabesques thickly worked in gold, and within the larger spaces in each corner-piece are the 'remains' of feathered caterpillars, now skeleton forms of threads only. The back of the book is particularly good, and most beautifully worked. It is divided into five panels, within each of which is a conventional flower, a cornflower alternating with a carnation, and the colours of all of these are marvellously fresh and effective. Among embroidered panelled backs it is probably the finest specimen existing.

Emblemes Chrestiens, par Georgette de Montenay. MS. à Lislebourg. [Edinburgh] 1624.

Charles I., when he was Prince of Wales, often used the book-stamps that had been cut for his brother Henry, and he also particularly liked the triple plume of ostrich feathers. It occurs, as has been shown, on one of Prince Henry's velvet-bound books, and it forms the central design on the satin binding of an exquisite manuscript written by Esther Inglis, a celebrated calligraphist, who lived in the seventeenth century. It is a copy of the *Emblemes Chrestiens*, by Georgette de Montenay, dedicated to Prince Charles, covered in red satin embroidered with gold and silver threads, cords, and guimp, with a few pearls, measuring $11\frac{1}{4}$ by $7\frac{3}{4}$ inches. In the centre is the triple ostrich plume within a coronet, enclosed in an oval wreath of laurel tied with a tasselled knot. A rectangular border closely filled with arabesques runs parallel to the edges of the boards, and there is a fleuron at each of the inner corners. In all cases the design is outlined in gold cord, and the thick parts of the design are worked in silver guimp. There are several spangles, and on the rim of the coronet are three pearls.

New Testament.   London, 1625.

One of the most curious embroidered satin bindings still left is now in the Bodleian Library, and a slightly absurd tradition about it says that the figure of David, which certainly is something like Charles I., is clothed in a piece of a waistcoat that belonged to that king.

It is a New Testament, printed in London in 1625, and covered in white satin, with a different design embroidered on each side. It measures $4\frac{1}{2}$ by $3\frac{1}{2}$ inches. On the upper board is David with a harp. He wears a long red cloak lined with

38—New Testament. London, 1625.

ermine, with a white collar, an under-garment
of pale brown, and high boots with spur-
straps and red tops. On his head is a royal
crown of gold with red cap, and he is playing
upon a golden harp. The face of this figure
resembles that of Charles I. The red cloak
is worked in needlepoint lace, and is in deep
folds in high relief. These folds are actually
modelled in waxed paper, the needlework being
stretched over them, and probably fixed on by
a gentle heat. The other parts of the dress
are worked in the same way, but without the
waxed paper, and the edges of the garments
are in some places marked with what might be
called a metal fringe, made in a small recurring
pattern.

David is standing upon a grass plot, represented by small arches of green purl, and before
him is sitting a small dog with a blue collar.
Above the dog is a small yellow and black pansy,
then a large blue 'lace' butterfly, on a chenille
patch, and a brown flying bird. Behind David
there is a tall conventional lily and a flying bird.
The sky is overcast with heavy clouds of red and
blue, but a golden sun with tinsel rays is showing
under the larger of them. On the lower board
is a representation of Abraham about to sacri-
fice Isaac. Abraham is dressed in a red under-
garment on waxed paper, in heavy folds with
a belt and edge of stamped-out metal, a blue

flowing cape and high boots, all worked in needle-point lace in coloured silks.

In his right hand he holds a sword, and his tall black hat is on the ground beside him. On the ground towards the left is Isaac in an attitude of prayer, his hands crossed, with two sheaves of firewood. He wears a red coat with a small blue cape. The ground is green and brown chenille. Above Isaac is a gourd, and above this a silver ram caught in a bush, on a patch of grass indicated by green purl. The sky is occupied by a large cloud, out of which leans an angel with wings, the hands outstretched and restraining Abraham's sword.

On the back are four panels, containing respectively from the top a butterfly, a rose, a bird, and a yellow tulip, all worked in needlepoint and appliqué. The pieces that are in high relief all over the book are edged with gold twist, and have moreover their counterparts under them closely fastened down to the satin. There are several gold spangles in the various spaces between the designs; the whole is edged with a strong silver braid, and there are two clasps with silver attachments.

Considering the high relief in which much of this work is done, the binding is in wonderful preservation, but many of the colours are badly faded, as it has been exposed to the action of light in one of the show-cases for many years.

39—New Testament and Psalms.   London, 1630.

Although no doubt it is advisable to expose many treasures in this way, it must be admitted that in the case of embroidered books it is frequently, if not always, a cause of rapid deterioration, so much so that I should almost think in these days of good chromo-printing it would be worth the while of the ruling powers of our great museums to consider whether it would not be wiser to exhibit good colour prints to the light and keep the precious originals in safe obscurity, to be brought out, of course, if required by students.

New Testament and Psalms.   London, 1630.

Several small English books of the seventeenth century were bound 'double,' *i.e.* two volumes side by side, so as to open different ways (compare p. 38). Each of the books, which are always of the same size, has a back and one board to itself, the other board, between them, being common to both. As already stated, this form of book occurs rarely in canvas bindings, and it is of commoner occurrence in satin.

A design which is frequently met with is well shown in the case of a double specimen containing the New Testament and the Psalms, printed in London in 1630, and covered in white satin, measuring 4¼ by 2 inches, the ornamentation being the same on both sides. In the centre, in

M

an oval, is a delicately worked iris of many colours in feather-stitch, the petals edged with fine silver cord. The oval is marked by a silver cord, beyond which are ornamental arabesques outlined in cord and filled in solidly, in high relief, with silver thread.

The backs are divided into five panels, containing alternately flowers in red, blue, and green silks, and star shapes in silver thread in high relief. Silver spangles have been freely used, but most of them have now gone; the edges of the leaves are gilt and gauffred in a simple dotted pattern. To the middle of the front edge of one of the boards is attached a long green ribbon of silk which wraps round both volumes.

Henshaw, *Horæ Successivæ.* London, 1632.

Henshaw's *Horæ Successivæ,* printed in London in 1632, is bound in white satin, and measures 4½ by 2 inches. It is very delicately and prettily worked in a floral design, the same on both sides, and is remarkable for its simplicity—a flower with stalk and leaves in the centre, one in each corner, and an insect in the spaces between them. The centre flower is a carnation, round it are pansy, rose, cornflower, and strawberry, while between them are a caterpillar, snail, butterfly, and moth. All of these are delicately worked in feather-stitch in the proper colours, and edged

40   Henshaw, Horæ Successivæ.   London, 1632.

41—Psalms. London, 1633.

all round with fine gold cord; the stalks are of the same cord used double. On the strawberries there is some fine knotted work.

The back is divided into four panels, containing a cornflower, rose, pansy, and strawberry, worked exactly in the same way as their prototypes on the sides. There were several gold spangles on sides and back, but many of them have been broken off, and on the front edges of each board are the remains of pale green ties of silk.

Psalms. London, 1633.

A copy of the Psalms, printed in London in 1633, is bound in white satin, embroidered in coloured silks worked in satin-stitch, and measures 3 by 2 inches. On the upper board is a gentleman dressed in the style of the period, with trunk hose of red and yellow, a short jacket of the same colouring, and a long, reddish cape. He has a broad-brimmed hat with coloured feathers, a large white collar, and a sword in his right hand. Near him is a beetle, and in the sky a blue cloud, and he is standing upon a grass mound. On the lower board is the figure of a lady in a deep pink dress, with white collar and cap. She holds a tall red lily in her right hand, and in the upper left-hand corner is a small cloud under which the sun is just appearing, and in the lower corner is a small flower. The lady is standing upon a small green mound. The outlines of both figures, as well as the inner divisions between the various garments, are marked with a gold or silver thread.

The back is divided into four panels, in which are a fly, a rose, a larger fly, and a blue flower. The outlines and legs of both the insects were marked originally with small pieces of peacocks' feathers, but the upper fly has lost most of these; the lower one, however, more ornamental, shows them clearly, and has the thorax still in excellent preservation, glittering with little points of green and gold. There is one broad ribbon of striped silk attached to the lower board.

This little book, which is in a wonderful state of preservation, has been always kept in the beautiful embroidered bag which I have described already on p. 16.

Psalms. London, 1635.

One of the most finely embroidered bindings existing on satin occurs on a small copy of the Psalms, printed in London in 1635, and measuring 3½ by 3 inches. The design is one which has been repeated in other sizes with small differences. There is a larger specimen at the Bodleian, but the British Museum example is the finer altogether.

On each side there is an oval containing an

42—Psalms.   London. 1635.

elaborate design most delicately worked in feather-stitch, the edges and outlines marked with very fine gold twist. On the upper board there is a seated allegorical figure with cornucopia, probably representing Plenty. Behind her is an ornamental landscape with a piece of water, the bright lines of which are feelingly rendered with small stitches of silver thread, hills with trees, and a castle in the distance. The other side has a similarly worked figure of Peace, a seated figure holding a palm branch; the landscape is of a similar character to that on the upper board, but the river or lake has a bridge over it. The work itself is of the same very delicate kind, the edges and folds of the dress being marked with fine gold twist.

Each of these ovals is marked by a solid framework with scrolls, strongly made with silver threads, and in high relief; in each corner is a very finely worked flower or fruit, pansy, straw-berry, tulip, and lily. The back is divided into four panels, a very decorative conventional flower being worked in each, representing probably a red lily, a tulip, a blue and yellow iris, and a daffodil. The edges of the boards are bound with a broad silver braid, the edges of the leaves are gilded and prettily gauffred, and there are remains of four silver ties.

Psalms. London, 1633.

There is often much speculation as to who
can have worked the English embroidered books,
and it is very rarely that any reliable information
on this interesting point is available.

There is, however, a manuscript note in a copy
of the Psalms, printed in 1633 and bound in embroidered white satin, that the work upon it was
done by 'Elizabeth, wife of Matthew Wren, Bishop
of Ely,' who was an uncle of the architect. The
volume still belongs to a member of the family,
Dr. W. T. Law of Portland Place, who has most
kindly allowed me to give an illustration of this
beautiful book. It measures 4 by 3 inches. The
design is different in details on each board, the
central design, however, being in each case contained within a strongly worked gold border in
high relief, widening out at each extremity into
a crownlike form, and richly augmented at
intervals with clusters of seed pearls. On the
upper board within the oval is a double rose with
curving stem, leaves, and a bud ; the petals are
worked in needlepoint, with fine gold twist at the
edges, and a cluster of pearls in the centre. In the
upper corners are a butterfly, with needlepoint
wings, and a bird, with needlepoint wing and tail.
In the lower corners are a unicorn and an antlered
stag, both recumbent, and in high relief.

On the lower board within the oval is a vine,

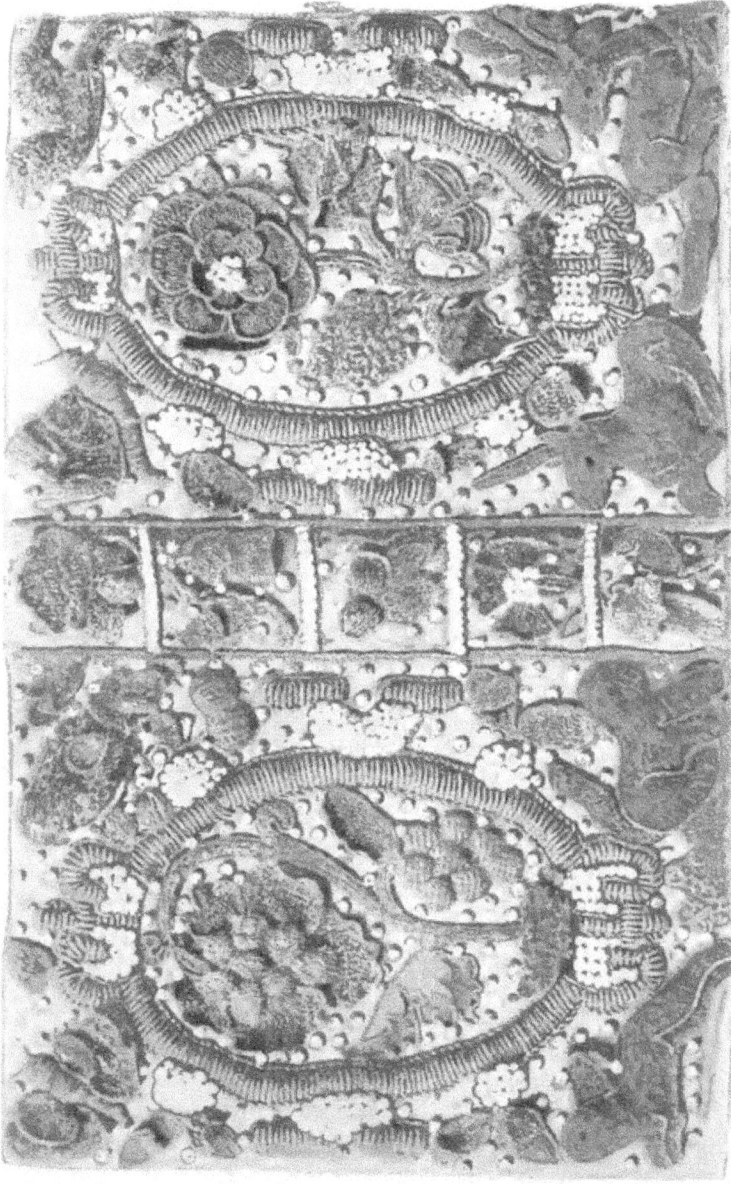

43 Psalms. London, 1633.

with curving stem and two large grape clusters, tendrils, and leaves, growing from a small green mound. The edges of the petals are bound with a fine gold twist, as are also the edges and outlines of the leaves, and most of these parts are worked in coloured silks, mixed with fine metal threads, in needlepoint lace-stitch.

A few hazel-nuts are scattered about outside the gold oval, and in each corner is a further ornamentation : a reddish butterfly with wings of needlepoint lace in relief and edged with a gold cord, a green parrot with red wings and tail, are in the two top corners, and in the two lower are a rabbit and a dog, each on a small green ground. Innumerable gold spangles are all over the sides and back, each kept in place by a small pearl stitched through.

The back is divided into five panels, by rows of pearls, and a conventional flower is in each, except the centre one which has an insect. These are all worked in needlepoint and edged with gold twist, the stems of some of them strongly made by a kind of braid of gold cords.

This little book is certainly one of the most ornamental specimens of any of the smaller satin-bound books of the seventeenth century, and although here and there some of the pearls are gone, altogether it is in very good condition, and it is rarely that such a fine example can now be met with in private hands.

Bible. London, 1638.

Several of the embroidered books on satin are worked chiefly in metal threads, and the designs on such books are not as a rule good. Whether the knowledge that the work was to be executed in strong threads has hampered the designer or not cannot be said, but certainly there is often a tinselly effect about these bindings that is not altogether pleasing.

In the case of a Bible printed in London in 1638, bound in white satin, and measuring 6 by 3 inches, one of the chief ornaments is a cherub's head, the face in silver and the hair and wings in gold. The working of this head and wings seems to me wrong. The face is, possibly enough, as well done as the material would allow, but the hair is made in small curls of gold thread, and the feathers of the wings are rendered in a naturalistic way with pieces of flat gold braid. This kind of realism is out of place in embroidery, and it is unfortunately characteristic of the English embroidered work of about this period, occurring generally on boxes, mirror frames, or the like, but only rarely on book-covers. The design is the same on both sides; a narrow arch of thick gold cord reaches about three-quarters up the side, and interwoven with it is a kind of cusped oval, with leaves, reaching up to the top of the book. The lower half of the arch

44—Bible. London, 1638.

is enclosed in a rectangular band of silver threads, broad and kept in place by transverse bars at regular intervals, and beyond it another row, made of patches of red and blue silk alternately. In the lower part of the oval is a ground of green silk, on which grow two double roses made of red purl. In the space enclosed between the top of the arch and the lower point of the oval is a bird worked in high relief in gold with a touch of red silk on his wings. Over the bird is a blue cloud, heavily worked in blue silk, and beneath is a small grass plot. The cherub's head already described is in the space between the top of the arch and the upper extremity of the oval; it is flanked by two small red purl roses. The two upper corners have undulating clouds in blue silk, and a red and yellow purl rose between them. There are several gold spangles all about, and innumerable small pieces of coloured purl.

The back is divided into four panels, in which are, alternately, a rose-tree on which are two red roses with yellow centres and green leaves, growing from a grass plot, and a blue rose with yellow centre and green leaves under a red cloud with silver rays. There are several spangles and some small pieces of coloured purl scattered about in the spaces.

The book is in excellent condition, owing, no doubt, to the fact that most of it is in metal, but it is representative of the lowest level to which the

N

art of the embroidered book in England has ever fallen.

Psalms. London, 1639.

A charming little piece of delicate workman-ship occurs in a copy of the Psalms, printed in London in 1639, and bound in white satin. It measures 3 by 2 inches. The design on each side is the same, but the work is slightly dif-ferent. A tall rose-tree, with gold stem, grows from a small chenille base, the rose petals beautifully worked in the finest of stitches, as well as the leaves, all of which are outlined with fine gold thread. From the lower branches of the rose-tree hang on one side a violet, and on the other a pansy, each worked in the same way as the rose, and edged with fine gold thread. The back is divided into four panels, containing respectively a cornflower, a pomegranate, a fruit, perhaps meant for an apple, and a honeysuckle, all conventionally treated and very delicately worked. The edge is bound all round with a strong braid, and there is one tie of broad, cherry-silk ribbon. With this book is its can-vas bag, embroidered in silver ground with coloured-silk flowers and tassels of silver, the general design and workmanship of which nearly resembles that of the finer bag already described at page 16. The silver has turned nearly black, as is usually the case with these bags.

45—Psalms.   London, 1639.

46—The Way to True Happiness.   London, 1639.

The Way to True Happiness.
London, 1639.

A copy of *The Way to True Happiness*, printed in London in 1639, is bound in white satin, and embroidered with figures of David and a Queen. It is a little larger than the majority of the satin-embroidered books, measuring 7 by 4½ inches, and is, for its time, a very fine specimen. Both figures stand under an archway with columns, all worked heavily in silver cord, guimp, and thread. The columns have ornamental capitals and a spiral running round their shafts, and the upper edge of the arch is ornamented with crockets of a peculiar shape. Within this archway, on the upper cover, is a full-length figure of a Queen, finely worked in split-stitch with coloured silks. She wears a red dress with long, falling sleeves, a purple body and gold collar. On her head is a golden crown, with six points. She carries, in her left hand, a golden sceptre, and has also a golden belt. The outlines are everywhere marked either with a gold or silver twist. On the ground, which is in small hillocks, grow a strawberry and two other small plants; a snail is also shown. Scattered about the field are a 'skeleton' caterpillar—at one time probably filled in with peacocks' feathers,—a conventional lily, a butterfly, and the sun, with rays, just appearing from under a cloud. In the two upper corners are flowers, a pansy and another, and smaller ones down each side.

On the lower board, within the arch, is a figure of David. He wears a short tunic of orange and silver, with vandyked edge, and a short skirt of blue and silver, with a long cloak of cream, pink, and silver, clasped with a silver brooch; on his head he wears a silver crown, with a red cap and green and red feathers; on his feet are brown, high boots. In his left hand is a silver harp of ornamental pattern, and in his right a silver sceptre with a little gold about it. The ground, in hillocks, has a few small flowers growing upon it, and a large tulip is just in front of the King; on the field are also a moth and a snail. At the top is a blue cloud. The upper corners have a red and yellow tulip and a pansy with bud in them, and smaller flowers are worked down each side. The back is very tastefully ornamented with an undulating scroll of gold cord, widening out here and there into conventional leaves of gold guimp in relief. On this scroll are sitting three birds, and there are also a bunch of grapes, a tulip, daffodil, and other flowers with leaves, conventionally treated, all worked in coloured silks.

There are the remains of two red and yellow silk ties on the front edges of each board, and the edges of the leaves are gilded and gauffred. With this book is a canvas bag,

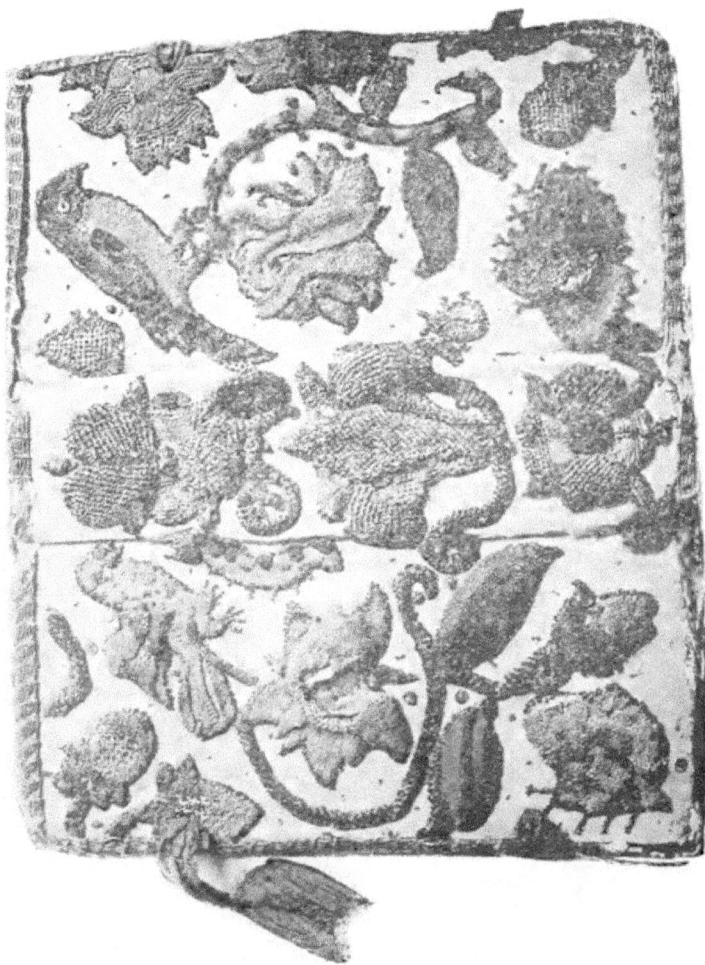

47 – New Testament. London, 1640.

simply ornamented with a design worked in red silk.

New Testament.   London, 1640.

The curious little New Testament of 1625, now at Oxford, which I have already described, is perhaps the earliest example left on which needle-point lace in coloured silks is much employed.

It occurs again largely on another small New Testament, printed in 1640, bound in white satin, measuring $4\frac{1}{2}$ by $2\frac{1}{4}$ inches; now in the British Museum. In this case the artist has not attempted the difficult task of producing a satisfactory figure in needlework, but has very properly limited her skill to the reproduction of flower and animal forms. On the upper cover is a spray of columbine, the petals of which, pink and blue, are each worked separately in needlepoint lace stitch, and afterwards tacked on to a central rib. The stalks and leaves of this spray are also worked in needlepoint, and on the top sits a bullfinch, worked in many colours in the same way, but fastened down close to the satin all round. In the corners are a beetle, a nondescript flower, a bud, and a butterfly with coloured wings in needlepoint, with replicas of them closely appliqués just underneath, on the satin. On the lower board is a spray of a five-petalled blue flower, the petals of which were originally worked in needlepoint and fastened on a central rib, but they have now all gone except two, leaving the rib of thick pink braid. The supporting replicas underneath are, however, perfect, showing what the original upper petals were like. This spray has two leaves, exquisitely worked in needle-point, and fastened by a stitch at one end, with the usual flat replicas underneath them, and there is also a bud. The stem is a piece of green braid. Above the spray is a parrot in needle-point, most of him fastened down round the edges, but his wings and tail left free. In the upper corner are two strawberries, and in the lower a butterfly, with coloured wings, left free in needlepoint. There are also two cater-pillars on this side.

On the back are three large flowers heavily worked in silk and metal threads, in needlepoint, and appliqués—a pansy, lily, and rose, with stalks of green braid. The boards are edged all round with a gold braid, and there are two green silk ties on each for the front edges. There are several gold spangles all about, but many more have gone. The work on both boards is very delicate, but that on the back is curiously coarse. Such imitative work as the needlepoint, which is perhaps seen at its best in the columbine, and the leaves on this book, is at all times a dangerous thing to use, except when it is only used as appliqué, as in the beautiful cover be-longing to this book, which I have described on

48—Psalms.   London, 1641.

page 18, and the work on which is very likely by the same skilled hand as that on the book. I believe this use of the needlepoint, or button-hole stitch, is only found in English work; it is exactly the same as is used on the old Venetian and other so-called 'point' laces, but executed in fine-coloured silk instead of linen thread, and without open spaces.

Psalms. London, 1641.

Nicholas Ferrar's establishment at Little Gidding in Huntingdonshire is often credited with having produced embroidered books, but there is really no authority for the belief. All the authentic bindings which came from Little Gidding have technical shortcomings from a bookbinding point of view, none of which are found on any embroidered books.

In the *History of the Worthies of England,* by Thomas Fuller, there is a short note about Little Gidding, and he says about the ladies there that 'their own needles were emploied in learned and pious work to binde Bibles.' This note and the mention of needles may have perhaps given the start to the belief that embroidered work was intended, but in all probability it only refers to the sewing of the leaves of the books upon the bands of the back, which is done with needle and thread. Moreover, the ladies of Little Gidding did actually sew the backs of their books in a needlessly elaborate way, putting in ten or twelve bands where three or four would have been ample. I also think that if embroidery had been intended by the sentence above quoted, it would have been more clearly mentioned. To 'emploie needles to bind Bibles' is hardly the description one would expect if the meaning was that when bound the Bibles were covered in embroidered work; but it may be safely interpreted as it is written, the sewing being a most important part of a book-binding, and one likely to be much thought of by amateur binders, as the nieces of Nicholas Ferrar were.

The attribution of embroidered bindings to Little Gidding may also have been strengthened by the fact that many of the bindings made there are in velvet, the ornamentation on which, though it is actually stamped in gold and silver, does to some extent suggest embroidery. Indeed, I have myself heard the remark, on showing one of these books, 'Oh, yes! Embroidery.'

Again, a peculiarity of the Little Gidding books is, generally, their large size, whereas the embroidered books, especially the satin ones, are usually very small.

One of the embroidered books thus wrongly credited to Little Gidding is a Psalter, printed in London in 1641. It is bound in white satin, very tastefully embroidered, the same design

49—Psalms. London, 1643.

being on each side, and measures 4 by 2 inches.
In the centre is a large orange tulip, shading from
yellow to red, finely worked in silks in shading-
stitch.   The stem is outlined in gold cord, and
has also symmetrical curves and leaves, some
of which are filled in with silver guimp.   The
flower is enclosed in an ornamental scroll and
leaf border, all made with gold threads and twists,
and having leaf forms in relief at intervals in
silver guimp.   The back has five panels, ornamented alternately with guimp scrolls and small
spheres of coloured silk.   There have been
spangles and small pieces of guimp scattered
about on the sides and back, but most of them
have gone.   There are no ties, and the edges of
the leaves are gilt, and have a small gauffred
pattern upon them.

The design of this book is extremely simple
and effective; the fine stitching on the tulip con-
trasts well with the strong metal border enclosing
it.   It may be considered a favourable specimen
of the commonest type of satin embroidered books
of the seventeenth century.   It is not in very
good condition.

Psalms.   London, 1643.

A very quaint design embroidered on white
satin covers a copy of the Psalms, printed in
London in 1643, and measuring $4\frac{1}{4}$ by $3\frac{1}{4}$

o

inches. On the upper side is a representation of Jacob wrestling with the angel, flanked by two trees with large leaves; the angel has wings and long petticoats. The lower board has a representation of Jacob's dream. The patriarch is asleep on the grass, his head upon a white stone, his staff and gourd by his side. He has pale hair and beard. Behind him is a large tree, and in front a conventional flower with leaves and bud, and from the clouds reaches a ladder on which are three small winged angels, two coming down, and one between them going up. Through a break in the clouds is seen a bright space, with rays of golden light proceeding from it.

The back is divided into five panels, in each of which is a flower. These resemble, to some extent, a red tulip, a lily, a red dahlia, a yellow tulip, and a red rose. The work here is not protected by any strong or metal threads, and it is consequently much worn. There are no signs of any tie ribbon, and the edges are plainly gilt.

Psalms. London, 1643.

Another copy of the Psalms, printed in London in 1643, bound in satin, and measuring $3\frac{1}{4}$ by $2\frac{1}{4}$ inches, bears on each side, within a circle, a miniature portrait of Charles I. worked in feather-stitch. The king wears long hair, moustache, and small pointed beard. He is

50—Psalms.   London, 1643.

crowned, and has a red cloak with miniver tippet, from under which appears the blue ribbon of the Garter worn round the neck, as it originally was, and having a small gold medallion attached to it. The initials C. R. in gold guimp are at each side. The circle is enclosed in a strong framework of silver cord and guimp in the form of four thin long pointed ovals of leaf form arranged as a diamond. The four triangular spaces between the diamond and the oval are filled with small flowers or small pieces of guimp and spangles. Towards each corner grows a flower, two pansies, and two others with regular petals. The remaining spaces are filled variously with green leaves, small patches of purl and gold spangles, and a strong gold cord encloses the whole. The back is divided into three panels, in each of which is an ornamental conventional flower, the upper and lower ones alike, and worked in shades of red with guimp leaves in relief, and the centre one with six petals worked in yellow and edged with a fine gold cord. There are no signs of ties ever having existed, and the edges of the leaves are gilt and slightly gauffred. It has been suggested that this little book may have belonged to King Charles I.; but the fact of his portrait being upon it is no proof of this, as portraits of this king are more numerous upon the bindings of English books than those of any other person.

Psalms. London, 1646.

The value of 'purl' was recognised some few years back, when I had some made, and explained its value and use to the Royal School of Art Needlework at South Kensington, and I believe they used it considerably.

On books the use of purl is generally auxiliary, but one small book bound in white satin, and measuring 4 by 2½ inches, a copy of the Psalms, printed in London in 1646, is entirely embroidered in this material, helped with gold braid and cord. The design is approximately the same on each side, a large flower with leaves in the centre, and a smaller flower in each corner. On the upper cover the centre flower is yellow and red, with two large green leaves, and the corner flowers are, possibly, intended for a cornflower, a jonquil, a lily, and a rose, but the material is so unwieldy that the forms are difficult to trace, and flowers worked in it are likely to assume forms that are unrecognisable, when finished, however well designed to start with. All the flowers and leaves are made with the purl cut into short lengths, drawn together at the ends by a thread run through, thus forming a succession of small arches. The stalks are made in gold cord. The flowers on the other side are, perhaps, a carnation in the centre, and round it a convolvulus, lily, daffodil, and rose. The back is divided into five

51- Psalms. London, 1646.

52 - Bible. London, 1646.

panels, in each of which is a 'purl' flower, all
worked in the same way, representing successively
a tulip, cornflower, carnation, lily, rose, or something analogous to them ; round the designs are
straight pieces of brown purl, and the edges are
bound with a broad gold braid. There are no
ties or signs of any, and the edges are simply
gilt. The purl is undoubtedly very strong ; I
possess a small patch-box worked on white satin
in a similar way to this little book, and although
it has been roughly used for some two hundred
and fifty years, the colour of the purl is still good ;
the upper surfaces of the small spirals, however,
show the copper wire bare almost everywhere.
The book, not having had anything like the hard
wear, is in very good condition, but it is too small
for the proper use of so much thick thread. The
larger leaves and petals are made in relief by
being sewn on over a few pieces of purl laid
underneath them at right angles.

Bible.   London, 1646.

A Bible printed in London in 1646 is bound
in white satin, and embroidered in coloured silks
and gold braid and cord, measuring 6 by 3½
inches. The same design is on both sides. In
the centre within an oval of gold braid and cord
is a spray of vine, with two bunches of grapes,
three leaves and a tendril, the fruit and leaves

worked in silk, and the stem in gold cord. Enclosing the oval is an arabesque design worked in gold cord and guimp, and at each corner is an oval of thin gold strips and gold cord; the gold strips are done in the manner known as 'lizzarding,' and are kept down by small stitches at intervals.

The back has four panels, in each of which is an arabesque design in coloured silks and gold cord or braid. Although this book is comparatively late, it is in a bad condition, and shows much wear; the design also is weak, and the workmanship inferior.

INDEX

PRINTED BY T. AND A. CONSTABLE, PRINTERS TO HER MAJESTY, AT THE UNIVERSITY PRESS, EDINBURGH: MARCH MDCCCXCIX